BIG OLLIE had a button nose, spit-curl bangs, toothbrush mustache, white gloves, a genteel manner and a slow burn.

SKINNY STAN had a triangular chin, unbrushable hair, a puzzled expression and a double take so funny it hurt.

Stan Jefferson got his start in the British music halls, Ollie Hardy as a boy singer in a Georgia minstrel troop. They were destined to become the universally beloved Laurel and Hardy, whose fans have included Joseph Stalin, Winston Churchill, Dylan Thomas, Charlie Chaplin and Tito.

This authentic biography portrays Laurel and Hardy as men as well as entertainers— men who were as warm, gentle and lovable off stage as on. The universal appeal of Laurel and Hardy is perhaps best summed up by Ollie Hardy himself when he said, "Those two fellows we created, they're nice, very nice people."

"Among many, Roach, Sennett, Lloyd, Langdon, Keaton, Fields . . . shine again in the book's pages.... He has captured the glow, mechanics and just plain fun of an era dead but ageless." *Hartford Courant*

Other SIGNET Biographies
You'll Want to Read

W. C. FIELDS: HIS FOLLIES AND FORTUNES
by Robert Lewis Taylor
A Pulitzer Prize-winning author chronicles the life of one of our century's funniest men, a man whose private adventures were no less hilarious than his masterful performances. Illustrated with photographs.
(#Q3064—95¢)

BOGIE *by Joe Hyams*
The biography of Humphrey Bogart, a great star in his lifetime and now a cult hero for a whole generation who never saw his films while he was alive, written by a close friend of the star, with the authorization and cooperation of Bogart's widow. Introduction by Lauren Bacall. Thirty-two pages of photographs.
(#T3071—75¢)

GREAT STARS OF HOLLYWOOD'S GOLDEN AGE
edited by Frank C. Platt
The true stories of the men and women behind the famous facades of Garbo, Valentino, Chaplin, Lombard, and John Barrymore. (#P2979—60¢)

LENA *by Lena Horne and Richard Schickel*
A great entertainer relates the dramatic story of her rise to stardom and her victory over fear and loneliness. (#T3015—75¢)

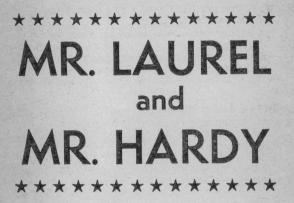

★ ★ ★ ★ ★ ★ ★ ★ ★ ★ ★ ★ ★ ★ ★ ★

MR. LAUREL
and
MR. HARDY

★ ★ ★ ★ ★ ★ ★ ★ ★ ★ ★ ★ ★ ★ ★

By John McCabe

*With a special foreword by
Dick Van Dyke*

A SIGNET BOOK

Published by
THE NEW AMERICAN LIBRARY

SIGNET TRADEMARK REG. U.S. PAT. OFF. AND FOREIGN COUNTRIES
REGISTERED TRADEMARK—MARCA REGISTRADA
HECHO EN CHICAGO, U.S.A.

SIGNET BOOKS are published by
The New American Library, Inc.,
1301 Avenue of the Americas, New York, New York 10019

PRINTED IN THE UNITED STATES OF AMERICA

ACKNOWLEDGMENTS

My prime obligation is to the dedicatee but I also give deep thanks to Lucille Hardy for the detailed information on Oliver Hardy; to the late Charley Rogers for his penetrating comments on the films; to Orson Bean for his views on comedy structure, and to Jack Benny, Eddie Cantor, the late Lou Costello, Henry Morgan, Marcel Marceau, and Groucho Marx for their ideas on Laurel and Hardy; to David Robinson for generously sharing his Laurel and Hardy preserves at the British Film Institute; to Denis Forman, former Director of the British Film Institute; to Buck Manbeck, Edward Kobus, and Mike Polacek the leading Laurel and Hardy film collectors in the country, for precious film clips; to Al Hine for the Dylan Thomas anecdote; to the British Film Institute and the Film Library of the Museum of Modern Art. I am also grateful for the aid extended by Mrs. James Arata, Richard Howard Brown, Frank Buxton, William K. Everson, Eda Laurel, Brown Meggs, Mrs. C. J. McCabe, W. T. Rabe, Mrs. Elizabeth Sage, Ben Shipman, Tom Sullivan, Bert Tracey, Ione Varden, and Basil Wright. And last I must give special thanks to Steve Allen who helped at a time when it was especially needed. I am eternally indebted to my old friend, John Carroll, for dragging me, a doubting child, to my first Laurel and Hardy film.

J.M.

CONTENTS

A Tribute by

DICK VAN DYKE*

Thirty years ago when the latest Laurel and Hardy movie played in my home town in Illinois I attended the Saturday matinees; that is to say from about 11 a.m. to maybe 9 or 10 p.m.—or whenever my mother and father came to drag me home.

From there on, and for the rest of the week, my parents were entertained, regaled, as were my friends at school by my impressions of Stan Laurel. But nobody really paid a lot of attention because every other kid on the block was doing his impressions of Stan Laurel. My father always did a pretty good impression of Stan; my son does a pretty good impression of Stan. You would have to go to a far corner of the world to find somebody who doesn't do an impression of Stan Laurel.

There are hundreds of millions of people all over the world who felt the pang of sorrow and sadness when Stan left us, and it's impossible for anyone to speak for all of those people. All I can do is speak for myself and say how I felt about him. Stan's influence decided me to go into show business in the first place and his influence molded my point of view, my attitude about comedy. I never of course had met the man, but four years ago, when I came to California I meant to meet Stan Laurel by hook or crook and I wangled for a year, any way I could, to get his phone number, his address—anything that could put me in touch with him. Do you know where I finally found it? In the phone book . . . in a West Los Angeles phone book: *Stan Laurel, Ocean Avenue, Santa Monica*. A teenage kid picked up the phone and received an invitation to come up there and visit, just the same as I did.

When Stan passed away, his little desk there was awash with fan mail that had been pouring in from all over the

* Taken from his funeral eulogy for Stan Laurel.

world as it had been during most of his later life; he insisted on sitting there, at that little portable typewriter and answering every one of them, personally, and of course he was so far back—months and months behind in the answering, but he wouldn't give up. He never gave up on anything; he never gave up on life and most of all, he never gave up that God-given mirth that he had.

In the wee small hours of one of his last mornings on earth, a nurse came into Stan's room to give him emergency aid. Stan looked up and said: "You know what—I'd lot rather be skiing." The nurse said: "Do you ski, Mr. Laurel?" He said: "No! But I'd lot rather be skiing than doing this."

Stan once remarked that Chaplin and Lloyd made all the big pictures and he and Babe made all the little cheap ones. "But they tell me," he said, "our little cheap ones have been seen by more people through the years than all the big ones. They must have seen how much love we put into them."

And that's what put Stan Laurel head and shoulders above all the rest of them—as an artist, and as a man. He put into his work that one special ingredient. He was a master comedian and he was a master artist—but he put that one ingredient that can only come from the human being, and that was *love*. Love for his work, love for life, love for his audience; and how he loved that public. They were never squares, or jerks to Stan Laurel.

Some of his contemporaries didn't criticize Stan favorably back in the thirties. Some of his contemporaries took great delight in showing their tools, and their skills, their methods, on the screen; they were applauded because the audience could see their art. Stan was never really applauded for his art because he took too much care to hide it, to conceal the hours of hard creative work that went into his movies. He didn't want you to see that—he just wanted you to laugh, and you did! You could never get him to pontificate about comedy. He was asked thousands of times, all through his life, to analyze comedy.

"What's funny?" he was always asked, and he always said: "How do I know? Can you analyze it? Can anybody?" He said: "All I know is just how to make people laugh."

That's all he knew!

Stan always believed that no comedy could merely depend on the spoken word, and all over the world, millions of people have laughed at Stan who never understood one word he ever said.

His sense of humor was clean and it was kind. The worst

things that ever happened in a Laurel and Hardy movie happened to Stan Laurel.

Stan was the creative one of the team, and the Babe liked that very much. His leisure hours were spent on the golf course. He was an easy-going, extroverted, happy man, and that was the way Ollie liked it. Stan found his fulfillment in the free hours which he spent at the studio—he loved working on new gags, on new ideas for comedy. Comedy was his whole life. Ollie had one well-known answer when anybody asked him about any of their current projects, he always said: "Ask Stan."

And that's a piece of advice that was still being taken during the last few years by every great comedian in this country, and all other countries around the world. They all came to "ask Stan." That living room in that small apartment has been graced in the last few years by Jerry Lewis, Danny Kaye, Marcel Marceau, Red Skelton, and dozens and dozens of others who just came up to "ask Stan." They all recognized him as the greatest of them all. His sweetness to me, I'll never forget. Stan didn't let them down either when they went up there. He was just as aware of the world around him in 1965 as he was at any other time in his life, and he knew what was funny about it—he saw what was funny about it too. And I can tell you, he could be the greatest today all over again.

I once tried to do an impression of Stan Laurel on my television show and I took meticulous care to get just the right kind of a hat, the right kind of clothes, and to get everything down right. I put it on the air, and in a fever after the show, I called him up and said, "What did you think?" He said, "It was just fine, Dicky, but ..." and for the next forty minutes, he gave me a list of details that I had done wrong. He was a perfectionist. And then he just said "God bless" and hung up. I wish I had a tape of that phone call: he said more things in there than I'll ever learn about my business or the importance of human beings being able to laugh at themselves. A man like Stan Laurel taught millions and millions of people to laugh at themselves. Somehow when we lose a great leader, a great scientist, a great teacher, there always seems to be somebody to take their place. But the loss that we had with a man like Stan Laurel is a deep one because there doesn't seem to be anybody to take his place. He won't happen again because the world's a different place now.

Three generations of people found his comedy equally human, warm and funny through his films, which he never owned, maybe future generations will; but he will never happen again and the world seems to know it. Telegrams and phone calls poured in from almost every country in the world, expressing love and affection and grief at the news that Stan had left us.

There were some strange places that Stan and Ollie went—they never took a vacation for a long time—but once they took a tourist vacation and went to China. They were in the deepest, deepest part of the interior of China and, as tourists, they visited a Buddhist temple there. They were invited to come in and look at the altar, and there on the altar was a tremendous blow-up in color of Ollie and Stan.

Once when they were in England—on a tour—they were surprised to find that wherever they went they were mobbed by crowds of people. They didn't realize how much everyone loved them so. They were hiding in Cobh, Ireland, to get some quiet, and suddenly, the church bells of Cobh began to ring—playing the Cuckoo Song and Stan said, "We both cried at that time, because of the love we felt coming from everyone."

Stan, of course, as most people know, spent the last years of his life with a serious illness. Those years were shared by his wonderful wife, Ida. She was the only one who really knew about the pain and suffering that was behind that famous smile, that wonderful high-pitched giggle he had. She shared his memories with him. He has a daughter, of course, Lois, and a son-in-law, Rand, and two grandchildren who had a better grandfather than Santa Claus could have been.

Stan and Ollie are both gone now and I feel the halls of heaven must be ringing with divine laughter at that sweet pair. I found something which was written on another subject but somehow seems to have been written for them:

What else had they been born for—it was their chance. With gay hearts, they gave their greatest gift and with a smile to think that after all they had something to give which was of value. One by one death challenged them; one by one, they smiled in his grim visage and refused to be dismayed. They had found the path that led them home and when at last they laid their lives at the feet of the Good Shepherd, what could he do, but smile.

A number of years ago I found a poem that I liked very

much and after I got to know Stan, I sent it to him a couple of Christmases ago as a Christmas card, and he called me and said how much he loved it and he was going to keep it. It's called "A Prayer for Clowns."

> "God bless all clowns
> Who star the world with laughter
> Who ring the rafters
> With a flying jest,
> Who make the world spin merry on its way
> And somehow add more beauty to each day.
> God bless all clowns
> So poor the world would be
> Lacking their piquant touch, hilarity,
> The belly-laughs, the ringing, lovely mirth
> That makes a friendly place of this earth.
> God bless all clowns—
> Give them a long good life,
> Make bright their way—they're a race apart!
> All comest most who turn their hearts' pain
> Into a dazzling jest to lift the heart.
> God bless all clowns."

I'd just like to say to Stan what he always said to all of us when we took his leave: God bless.

MR. LAUREL

The sixteen-year-old boy who was to become internationally famous as a pleasant, dim-witted troglodyte stood nervously in the wings of the tiny Glasgow theater pulling at his crop wig and twitching his heavily rouged nose. Something more than ordinary stage fright was giving Arthur Stanley Jefferson a severe case of nerves. In making his stage debut at Pickard's Museum, he had played hookey from work. This did not seem to him particularly reprehensible inasmuch as his employer was also his father, and parents have a way of coming around to reason on matters like this. Nevertheless, as he shakingly brushed off his trousers, the vision of his father did come to him and a stern, admonitory vision it was.

The trousers were his father's. Not just his trousers; they were his finest double-checked trousers which he wore to race meetings and which he fancied, in the Runyon phrase, more than somewhat. They were, at the moment, basically the same trousers with one interesting exception: to fit a sixteen-year-old, they had been cut off at the bottom—cut off crudely—and with fashionable cuffs truncated, they had become the typical baggy pants of the English music hall comedian. For that was what young Arthur Stanley Jefferson desired above all else in life: to "go on the halls" and become another Dan Leno, to strut to the upswing of a loud, solid-beat pit band, to tell a few uproarious jokes, to sing a song or two with beautifully wrought punch lines that whipped the audience into a frenzy of laughter, and then, to dance off, hat high, with applause coming to warm him like the south wind.

Arthur Jefferson, the owner of the trousers, might well have understood his son's dreams. He was himself of the theater, having written, produced, and acted in plays in the North of England during the latter decades of the nineteenth century. Originally the lessee of theaters in Bishop Auckland, Tynemouth, Blyth, Jarrow, Hebburn, and Wallsend, he had come in 1905 to Glasgow as manager of the Metropole, a famous theater which had originally known glory as the Old

Scotia. A.J., as Arthur Jefferson was known, loved the Metropole as he loved all the theaters he managed. His versatility in show business was proverbial in English theatrical circles. He not only wrote plays for himself but for other leading actors as well. He had married a beautiful actress, Madge Metcalfe, the Theda Bara of her day in North England's theatrical world. In addition to writing and directing most of his plays and sketches, he booked them on various circuits to tour all of the island. In *Up the Years from Bloomsbury*, George Arliss, who played as a juvenile in one of the companies in which A.J. was prominent, says of him: "Arthur Jefferson, who played the character parts, used to make everything. He made his own wigs and even his grease paints, and from him I learnt many tricks of which I should otherwise have remained ignorant."

In later years, Stan still retained vivid memories of his father. "He was of medium height, and I guess I inherited his red hair, which was always kept in a crew cut. He was a very energetic man, a stylish dresser, and was always referred to as 'The Guv'nor.' He was a great showman. Had a unique flair for advertising his theaters and shows. He pulled some unusual stunts. I can remember once he had a lion cage hauled around the streets with a real lion in it mauling a body. The body wasn't real, of course—just a fully dressed dummy with a big piece of meat inside. When crowds would gather around the wagon, canvas signs would drop down reading, *Tonight! At The Theatre Royal!*

"Another stunt was to have a hansom cab driving around with a chap in evening dress, seemingly dead, with a dagger in his chest, bleeding heavily, and the cabby unaware of the situation. This would be advertising a horror show. Or once in a while, Dad would have a balloon released and, at a certain height, smoke would come out, people would gather and then a big advertising banner would drop out and hang there. He was universally loved by all the townspeople in whatever place he worked. He was charitable to the poor, giving shoes and stockings to poor kids who couldn't afford them. He also arranged special matinees many times for the inmates of the poorhouses, pick them up in buses, and when they left the show, he gave them all packages of tea, sugar, cookies, tobacco, and snuff. He liked everybody and everybody liked him. I think that's why he was such a good showman."

In view of these remarkable indications of A.J.'s knowledge and love of the theater, it would seem less than unlikely that his son should have any qualms about obtaining his father's approval of his entry into the theater. Yet the forbidding vision of A.J. remained strong and clear to young Stan as he rubbed his knuckles and looked out at the act now occupying stage center. A.J. was a good, a kind, indeed a bountiful father, but like all fathers, he had limits.

Stanley, being born into a peripatetic profession, had to take his schooling on the road, as it were. Despite this, his father insisted on sending him to the best schools in Gainford, Bishop Auckland, and Tynemouth. The Jefferson family, mother, father, three sons, and a daughter were close—but at a distance. The boys, Gordon, Everett, and Stanley, followed close on the heels of their busy father whose various theaters claimed his attention continually. There were side excursions for them to various boarding schools at times, and the girl, Beatrice Olga, was spared much of this rushed existence because she spent a great deal of her childhood in convent school. "I suppose we had very little of what you'd call family life," Stan recalls. "We were very seldom all together. I was almost always either in boarding school or living with my grandparents in Ulverston where I was born, but still, strange as it may seem, we were always a close family." When the family moved more or less *en bloc* to Glasgow in 1905, Stan was sent to Ruther Glen School and from there to Queen's Park Academy. Here at Queen's Park, where Stan was to end his schooling, commenced a pattern of familiar experiences.

Young Stan, to put it minimally, was not fond of school. Initially, he had wanted to try it because he had observed the splendid collar-and-coat his older brother always wore on school days. But after obtaining his own raiment in course of time, Stan found that school was the last place on earth he wanted to be. "There I was," he says of himself then, "all dressed up with absolutely no place to go!" At Queen's Park, he hit upon a device for playing hookey that was effective for him and profitable for the teacher. Once when Stan was ill, his father wrote him a note of excuse to the master of the form and enclosed a few complimentary tickets to the Metropole. Stan, knowing where the *Complimentary* rubber stamp was kept, proceeded to manufacture a number of wonderful free afternoons for himself. On these glorious days he would go fishing or back home to play. On one occasion, his father returned home unexpectedly. "And what the hell are *you* doing here?" A.J. demanded. The magic rubber stamp was hidden.

That he did not stay in school, that he was able to convince A.J. that schooling was a Procustean horror was not only a tribute to his own persistence and powers of pleading but to the clearheadedness of A.J. as well. "Well, lad," A.J. told him, "if you can't take any more of school, I'll give you a job taking care of the gallery box office. You'll tot up the take after each performance and bring the accountings downstairs to me."

Stan totted up and took accountings down but he possessed C.P.A. instincts in no greater measure than he did a scholar's. A.J. was not greatly upset over the boy's ignorance of rudimentary mathematics. He knew that from sheer exposure Stan would master the intricacies of a box-office statement. In the meantime, let him have his fun. Let him go backstage as he always did during each show. Let him dress in silly costumes and talk ceaselessly to the comedians and repeat their jokes at the dinner table. He would get over it in time and become a theater manager who knew the business—to become, at last, the one person in show business who, given a level head and at least nominal ability in booking, always made money: the man who ran that part of the theater in front of the footlights. A.J. loved to act and write and direct (he was a superior comedian), but he knew that only too frequently the deeds of the actor are written in water, and he did not hesitate to say so.

The essence of these things was running through Stan's brain as his cue impended. God knows this isn't the greatest theater in the world, he thought, but it's my start, and it had better be a good start. Pickard's was a fascinating, heterogeneous show place which was at once a side show, museum, and penny gallery featuring peep shows, or penny-winders as they were then known in Scotland. For a ha'penny, one could play the gramophone machine (the wonder of the day in those parts), take a look at the stuffed seal, or (forbidden delight) see what the butler saw in thirty exciting seconds at the penny-winder. Then, unsurfeited by these pleasures, one could walk into another room of minuscule proportions boasting a tiny stage at one end. There were no seats. A small ladies' orchestra of three pieces trilled and shrilled while the patrons stood and watched. As wretchedly inadequate as this was, this was a *theater*—people paid to see you—and it was here that Stan some days before had approached Albert E. Pickard, the Mr. Show Business of Glasgow, owner of this and more elevated enterprises, to plead for a "try-on."

Pickard at the time was a picture of the typical prosperous theatrical entrepreneur at the turn of the century. Short, stocky, sporting a splendid Vandyke beard and its wedded mate, a cutaway suit, Pickard had just the right air of sporty affluence so characteristic of the impresario. "He was a fascinating man," Stan recalls today. "He had money then, of course, but nothing like what he accumulated later. Later on, he bought some film houses and they brought him money, too. One time he had trouble with an advertising firm. They couldn't seem to get up enough billboards to advertise his shows so he bought a great many vacant lots around the city for peanuts in order to put up his own boards. As the years rolled by, the lots became valuable property and he eventually made a million on them. He's retired now and is a great philanthropist. I see him every time I get back to Glasgow and he's still the same friendly person, although now the beard is gone and he wears the kilt instead of the cutaway. And he's got a thick Scots brogue which is delightful because he came to Glasgow as a young man straight from the East End of London. He's an out-and-out Cockney. But I'll always remember him best as I saw him that first day when I asked him for a job."

On that day, Pickard asked him why he wanted a trial turn.

"I'm funny," Stan said simply.

"How d'ye know?" asked Pickard without an eye blink.

"Let me on just once, sir," Stan pleaded, "and if I'm not any good, then I shan't pester you anymore. But I *will* be good. You'll see. And if I'm any good, maybe you'll give me a chance at your hall in Clydebank?"

After Pickard learned that this slim, rather solemnly handsome young man was the son of a prominent showman, he gave him the chance. Not much to lose if he turned out badly; and if he did half well, perhaps . . . who could tell?

These thoughts and more were turning Stan Jefferson's brain into a cat's cradle of worry as he stood in the wings. He had been waiting for hours, it seemed. He felt he could do it. He *knew* he could do it. But . . .

"Jefferson! You're on! Hop it!"

And on he was. This was excitement beyond the power of dreams. As he slithered out into the middle of the stage in a sliding eccentric dance, thanking God that at least A.J. wasn't there to see him make a proper, ruddy fool of himself, he turned, faced the audience, opened his mouth to sing—and did the first of a long line of notable double-takes.

There, across the room, leaning against the doorway next to Pickard was A.J.

There was not time now to accommodate the varying emotions of despair, hope, and defiance that surged through him. Time now only for the show and the act. The act was perhaps as thorough a melange of stolen gags, dances, and weird witticisms as has never been seen in a British music hall anywhere any time. For months, Stan had been watching some of the cleverest "boy" comedians in the halls. These youths, a special type of comedian now long out of fashion, played as "singles," purveying a mixture of dances and jokes best (and perhaps mercifully) described as inimitable. Stan admired them immoderately. For one thing, they were headliners: Laddie Cliff, Boy Glen, Nipper Lane (later to become famous as Lupino Lane), and others. They had no greater admirer than this Lancashire lad who watched them night after night without tiring, taking notes on their movements and dances, memorizing every vocal inflection, jotting down many of their jokes for his own delight and eventual use. From these jokes, and some of his own, he had extracted enough to form the nucleus of his own routine, and had paid a precious half crown to a Glasgow musician for an original song. This was the act which he was performing with urgent vigor before the eyes of his father, Mr. Pickard and a few scattered patrons of the Museum Music Hall.

"The act was awful," Stan admits, "just bloody awful. But I finished strong. And what's more, the applause was very big. I didn't realize that this was because the audience felt sorry for me. I figured that out for myself later on. At any rate, it was my first time before a live audience, and I felt good. I went backstage just on top of the world. Then as I started to take off my make-up, it hit me. I was going to have to face my dad. I got dressed, took a tram home, and just as it was going by the Metropole, I decided to swing off and face him then and there. I knew I'd have to face it sooner or later. I walked up the long flight of stairs and I dreaded every second of it. Those stairs never seemed so long before. I came to the outside of his office, and I could see his shadow behind the glass. It looked awfully big, that shadow. I knocked and he said, 'Come in.' Dad just looked up at me sharply, paused for a few seconds and then said, 'Well, congratulations. Sit down. Want a whiskey and soda?' I just gaped at him for a moment and then I really made a proper fool of myself. I burst into tears."

A.J. told the boy gently that he did not have any objection

to the stage as a livelihood—how could he?—*if* Stan was sure he wanted it. Stan was sure. And by the bye, A.J. wanted to know, where had he picked up that gorgeous pair of checked trousers? Stan sobbed out the truth and A.J. took the news not perhaps with full equanimity but at least in a spirit of comparative moderation.

The career of Stan Laurel (the Laurel was to be acquired later by accident in the United States) had begun. A.J. gave him a letter to Levy and Cardwell, producers of a pantomime company then touring England in *Sleeping Beauty*. The year was 1907.

For Stan, 1907 was the dividing year between boyhood and manhood. Looking back at that year, he can recall the stir and rush of the Edwardian age. There were broughams carrying top-hatted gentlemen and fur-encircled ladies to the theater past scenes of unendurable poverty. The gayest monarch since Charles II sat on the British throne when he was near it, but as usual, during much of 1907 he was not near it. He was paying more or less official visits to Paris, Madrid, and Rome. Colonialism was having its problems even then in the form of a solemn conclave, the Third Imperial Conference in London. There was peace talk that year (the Second Peace Conference at The Hague); discussion with Russia about the sphere of influence in the Near East (British-Russian Convention on Persia); there was social upheaval (2500 suffragettes demonstrated in Hyde Park); and there was progress (wireless telegraph service for newspapers between England and America was initiated). A changing world, but in the new world, the world of comedy that Stan Laurel was entering, time was timeless. Here, the old was always singularly new, and vice versa. Comedy, like tragedy, is a country without boundaries and an age without years. In joining the *Sleeping Beauty* pantomime, Stan came into comedy and comedy took him for its own.

One of the stars of *Sleeping Beauty* was Wee Georgie Wood, the pint-sized comedian, who in 1959 was still touring in pantomime. Stan, at a salary of a pound a week, played one of the Golliwogs who stood by the cradle of the baby (Wee Georgie). He stood patiently. He didn't move a muscle all through the first act. Clearly, this did not afford much scope for one who was burning to foot it and jest it about in livelier company, but he held his patience. At least he was a paid member of a professional company, and he had some measure of added importance as assistant stage manager and call boy. He was in the theater all the way.

Following the *Sleeping Beauty* season, he went on as a single again à la Pickard for a few odd engagements, and understudied for *Home from the Honeymoon,* a sketch by A.J. then current on the Moss Empire Circuit. The year after, he joined a company which was touring a deathless offering by Hal Reed called *Alone in the World.* The play is worthy of mention not only because it gave Stan Laurel his first comedy-character part on any stage but also because it shows what theatergoers of the day would accept in the name of serious drama.

Alone in the World opened with Stan, whose adolescent features were not quite disguised by a Joe Jackson tramp make-up, fishing on the banks of a levee in the Deep South. The deep-in-Dixie effect was somewhat vitiated by a back-drop of the Brooklyn Bridge stretching out to infinity. To make the total aspect even more delightfully bizarre, a chorus was heard offstage singing softly and insistently, "Way down upon the Suwanee River . . . far, far from home." Stan listened to this for an impatient moment or two following curtain rise, threw away his fishing pole and in a piping but assertive voice uttered a classic line: "Wal, I guess 'n' calculate I can't ketch no fish with that tarnation mob a-singin'. *(Pause)* Gee whizz!" Stan remembers this line word for word and often wishes that he did not.

He is glad that he does not remember much of the plot, but the play added to his maturity by making him aware early in his career that the theater can promise the patron much and pay out little. He has a vivid recollection of the standard poster used by the *Alone in the World* company to advertise its quality. The billing, depicting one of the climactic scenes in the play, was a picture of an expensive and expansive executive suite, oak-paneled, with a luxurious desk dominating the room. A harried banker sat at the desk with his head buried in his hands while a large mob shouted for its money in the Corinthian waiting room outside. What the audience actually saw during the play was a tiny box-set approximately 4 by 6 yards, a cardboard safe, a rickety table, and before it, the banker seated on a kitchen chair. A noise of two company members "off," shouting loudly, under-scored the dramatic entrance into the scene of the property man, the stage manager, and Stan (with make-up removed), constituting another large portion of the "gigantic" mob besieging the bank. These three chanted in unison: "We want our money! We want our money!"

Stan points out that the chant was heartfelt. The players had not been paid for weeks. Early in the tour, the play's title attained full significance for the cast. The manager skipped; Stan went home to rest.

Some months later, he joined Fred Karno's well-known troupe of music hall artists playing at the Hippodrome in Manchester. Karno is important to the history of film comedy—much more so than he ever imagined. It was Karno who afforded, indirectly, the opportunity for the pantomime talents of both Charlie Chaplin and Stan Laurel to develop and attain first bloom. Fred Karno should not be forgotten.

Karno's real name was Fred Wescott. His most vital contribution to British music hall history was the wordless play, the pure story-pantomime, of which *Jail Birds* and *Mumming Birds* were the most notable. Karno, a short, well-built man of brimming energy, was to become the most successful showman in England. "There was no one like him," Stan remembers. "He had no equal. His name *was* box-office. He was a great boss, kindly and considerate—and I hate to remember how he turned out eventually. He made a lot of money, and he deserved it. Well, his last venture was his downfall. After he had made such a great name for himself and a lot of money, he bought an island in the Thames. He had a big hill on it smoothed away, and built a large hotel on the site as a weekend resort with a large restaurant, tennis courts, golf course, and all that. He called it The Karsino, and he hired Jack Hylton's band and hundreds of people for the staff. He had a great opening. All show business on the British Isles came to it and it looked like a mint—but he forgot one thing: the weather. After the hit opening, it rained and rained and rained all through that summer season. It drained him financially. That terrific overhead for the one season eventually ruined him. He went broke and finally wound up running a little retail wine and beer shop in the south of England and died shortly after that. It was a real tragedy. But when I knew him at the time I joined his company, he was on top of the world."

When Stan joined the *Mumming Birds* company in Manchester, it had already become the most famous act in the halls. *Mumming Birds* (known in the United States as *A Night in an English Music Hall*) was one of the most fantastically funny variety acts ever known. Whenever old troupers from English variety or American vaudeville gather, *Mumming Birds* is spoken of as probably the greatest single ensemble act of the century.

The theater curtain rises on a false proscenium flanked by four empty theater boxes, two on each side of the stage. Stage center is a tab curtain which is drawn to reveal the acts-within-the-act. Overture begins and people enter the four boxes, bowing, shaking hands, laughing. Into the box downstage right now comes the actor identified in the program as The Boy—wearing Eton collar and suit—accompanied by his uncle, a staid old man. The Boy is an extraordinarily cocky type, always carrying with him a great supply of Bath buns, bananas, nuts, and sweetmeats which he not only devours summarily throughout the act but also uses for pelting purposes when some of the unfortunate "artistes" appear. The last of the spectators to enter is The Drunk, in impeccable evening attire, who appears in the box downstage left. The Drunk was played initially by Billy Reeves and later by Charlie Chaplin. When Chaplin played the part, Stan Laurel understudied him, but never played the role.

An usherette precedes The Drunk and shows him his seat. He takes his right glove off, swaying delicately, tips the girl and then begins to peel the glove again from his bare right hand. The girl points out his error and leaves as he selects a cigarette from his case and attempts to light it from an electric light bulb just outside the box. He is infuriated at the failure of the cigarette to function and is about to commit violence when he notices that The Boy has lighted a match which he now holds out. The Drunk smiles, bows gracefully, and in leaning forward to get his light, falls out of the box and sprawls on the stage.

The performance is about to begin. The Drunk clambers back as the number one card bearing the legend THE COMIC SINGER is placed on the easel. Stan was usually The Comic Singer. All of the "inner" acts were designed to be uniformly horrible for a twofold purpose: the entertainment of the actual audience and the disedification of The Drunk who pantomimed a wide series of reactions to each act. The Comic Singer sings an unfunny song in a heart-rending voice, and for an encore tells some magnificently unfunny jokes. A typical one:

"You know, the last time I sang this song a fellow said to me, 'You've got a wonderful voice. You ought to be with Carl Rosa.' 'But Carl Rosa's dead,' I said. 'Yes, I know,' said the fellow, 'that's what I mean!' "

The Drunk reacts to this with spirited indignation and chases The Comic Singer offstage. He returns quickly, flicks the number one card off the easel to reveal number two THE WOMAN SOPRANO, who, in her way, is equally dreadful and again incurs The Drunk's wrath, and is disposed of by him in somewhat similar fashion. The Magician follows with several lamentably inadequate tricks, followed by The Quartet, a group of rustics who sing interminable choruses of "Hail, Smiling Morn That Tips the Hills with Gold." The Drunk subjects them to rigorous insult and they are replaced by The Topical Vocalist who sings songs of heroes or news events of the day. (Winston Churchill and his adventures were popular topics at the time Stan joined the company.) The more ridiculous the song, the funnier to the audience and the more infuriating to The Drunk they became.

The Topical Vocalist was followed by The Wrestler, announced by a gentleman in evening dress, as "Marconi Ali, the Terrible Turk, the Greatest Wrestler Ever to Appear Before the British Public." The Turk appears, under-fed, scraggy-lean, accoutered in fez and giant mustache, flexing his rubber-band muscles. The Boy throws a bun before The Wrestler who leaps forward and devours it ferociously much to the announcer's embarrassment. The announcer flails at him and shouts, "Back, Ali, back, back! And now, ladies and gentlemen, I wish to make an offer unprecedented in the annals of British sportsmanship. The management is proud to make an offer of £100—yes £100—to anyone in the theater who is able to throw Marconi Ali in the space of fifteen seconds. Who will take him on?" A plant from one of the top boxes yells, "I'll take him, Guv!" and the audience applauds frantically. "How do I get down?" yells the plant. "Jump!" shouts The Boy. While the challenger is making his way down by orthodox means, a carpet is spread before The Wrestler who flexes his puny arms, ignoring the elaborate "takes" of The Drunk. The challenger enters, throws his coat over the Drunk's arm which is extended over the box railing. The Drunk throws it off, the challenger throws it back. This ends in an on-off sequence culminating in a wrestling match between The Drunk and the challenger, resulting in the challenger being thrown off the stage entirely. The Drunk now prepares to fight The Wrestler and in his excessive enthusiasm begins to take off his clothes. He is hustled offstage and returns a few moments later in long underwear tastefully decorated with red ribbons. The fight begins again and The Drunk finally throws The Wrestler by tickling him into surrender. The entire act then ends in a melee of gigantic proportions with all participants engaged in a simultaneous series of ructions: hooting, fighting, food-throwing, ripping of clothes.

This ending was typical of the one weak spot in most Karno shows. They played beautifully and to extravagant laughter but they usually sagged at the end. *Mumming Birds* was a spectacular success, notwithstanding. The various "inner" acts were changed constantly for fear of piracy by other music hall acts, but the frame of The Boy and The Drunk as the basic "outside" comedians never varied.

Mumming Birds is important in the consideration of Stan Laurel's ability as a comedian. It was, above all else, mime—and mime was to become absolutely indigenous to the Laurel style. For Stan Laurel and other great exponents of the art, the craft of the mimic is based on direct human observation—in a study of the body at work doing what it always does—isolating the moments of human function that are beautiful or ludicrous and reproducing them to stir the beholder to rapture or laughter. Mime is a hard school and its apprentices must feel and know every inch of flesh and bone in the learning process. The *Mumming Birds* experience showed young Stan that a simple gesture, effectively and directly performed without tricks and closely following the pattern of nature, is always funnier than clever words or funny songs. It was this basic dependence on mime that made Stan Laurel and Charlie Chaplin ideal comedians for the silent films.

At one time or other, Stan essayed almost all the parts in *Mumming Birds*. He learned by experiment and observation that a laugh can be built to almost double its original intensity by a formidable reaction of shock or surprise, a "take"—and that *this* laugh could be topped by a good, freewheeling "double-take." He discovered that good takes are as basic to good comedy as salt to stew. The comedian can get along without them but things are not nearly so good as they might be with their judicious application. They heighten and indeed channel audience reaction to humor. In the later development of the dim-witted character in the Laurel and Hardy films, Stan Laurel was to develop the take to such a fine point that he was able to pull it inside out and invert it deliberately for added comic effect.

Mumming Birds, then, was the best acting academy any comedian could ever attend. The company made successful tours all over Britain, and in September 1910 came to the United States. Sponsored by the Sullivan-Considine Empress circuit, Karno's troupe played the major American cities to great acclaim but the younger people found that touring America was not wholly pleasurable. Even before they landed they were aware that it would represent a vivid contrast to their own way of life. For one thing, their salary would not go nearly so far in the States as it would at home. To at least one member of the company, America was a welcome challenge.

On the cattle boat carrying the troupe, young Charlie Chaplin astonished the company one morning as they sat on deck watching the shores of the United States come into view. He leaped to his feet, rushed to the railing and declaimed loudly: "America, I am coming to conquer you! Every man, woman and child shall have my name on their lips—Charles Spencer Chaplin!" He bowed low to the friendly hootings of the company and sat down with vast aplomb. If any of America's millions had seen the offstage Charles Spencer Chaplin of 1910, they might well have joined in the Karno troupe's derisive comments on his forecast of future greatness. "He was a very eccentric person then," says Stan. "He was very moody and often very shabby in appearance. Then suddenly he would astonish us all by getting dressed to kill. It seemed that every once in a while he would get an urge to look very smart. At these times he would wear a derby hat (an expensive one), gloves, smart suit, fancy vest, two-tone side button shoes and carry a cane. I have a lot of quick, little memories of him like that. For instance, I remember that he drank only once in a while and then it was always port. He read books incessantly. One time he was trying to study Greek, but he gave it up after a few days and started in to study yoga. A part of this yoga business was what was called the 'water cure'—so for a few days after that, he ate nothing, just drank water for his meals. He carried his violin whenever he could. Had the strings reversed so he could play left-handed, and he would practice for hours. He bought a cello once and used to carry it around with him. At these times he would always dress like a musician, a long, fawn-colored overcoat with green velvet cuffs and collar and a slouch hat. And he'd let his hair grow long in back. We never knew what he was going to do next. He was unpredictable.

"We had a lot of fun in those days. Charlie and I roomed together and I can still see him playing the violin or cello to cover the noise of the cooking of bacon I was doing on the gas ring (forbidden, of course). Then we'd both take towels and try to blow the smoke out of the window. I remember one funny incident in those early days just after we landed in the States. I suppose you know that in English hotels guests leave their shoes outside the door when they retire so that the porter can give them a polish during the night. I did that as a matter of course the first night we landed in the States in our New York hotel. The next morning I got up, went to the door, looked out—and no shoes. I went down to the desk clerk mad as hell and demanded to know what had become of my shoes. When I had explained where I had put them, the man wanted to know why in the hell I had done *that*. I explained but it didn't do any good. My shoes were stolen— and to show you my financial situation at the time, they were the only shoes that I owned! So—and this is true—I actually walked over to the theater fully dressed, wearing my slippers. I'll never forget those slippers. They each had a single candle painted on them, and running around the glow of light from the candles were the words, *Good Night*. Good night is right!

"We must have been funny-looking chaps what with our English style of dress and speech. I remember one time Charlie and I were walking over to the theater all dressed up, hanky up the sleeve, spats, double-breasted coat, carrying canes—and on the way there we became aware of Nature's urgent call. Now, public conveniences are a regular part of English life, but they certainly aren't in America. We searched high and low and couldn't find accommodation. Finally, in desperation, we asked a cop where the nearest public convenience was. 'The nearest what?' yelled the cop. We asked again, very politely. He finally got our drift and said very loudly, 'Aw, hell, you'll have to go to a saloon, mister!' Mind you, we were now in a pretty anxious state. We got to a saloon and started down the aisle, as it were, when we realized that we hadn't purchased anything to warrant our use of the facilities. These polite Englishmen. So, tortured as we were, we marched up to the bar very bravely, ordered a beer and sipped it for a few seconds before we flew away."

It was while in New York that the forebodings of the supporting people in the company were realized. Living expenses were considerably higher than they were in England, and the United States of 1910 did not much resemble the England of 1910. It was still a pioneer country in many ways: both New Mexico and Arizona were two years away from attaining the dignity of statehood. There was still the rawness of the Old West not only on its home ground but all over the country. The United States was far from its cruelly civilized, atom-dominated near-maturity; it was young— ready and willing to grow in all ways. The affable William Howard Taft was the occupant of 1600 Pennsylvania Avenue in Washington, D.C. It was a naïve time, a warm time, a time so far and so near to war. To the young people in the Karno troupe, the newness and the warmth of the country were puzzling. And if the increase in living costs was unwelcome so too were the unusual and inequitable conditions of theatrical touring.

The odd routing of the newly rechristened *A Night in an English Music Hall* company through the States found them making big jumps from engagement to engagement. They were not paid during travel periods. These conditions made touring almost impossible for many of the supporting performers to endure, and Stan, not receiving the raise he wanted, left Karno in Colorado Springs together with Arthur Dandoe, who played The Magician and The Announcer in the act. Dandoe was an excellent character actor and comedian. He had an instinct for comedy much like Stan's, and the two of them whiled away their time back to England in the creation of their own original act.

The result was *The Rum 'Uns from Rome*. Compounded of music hall slapstick and traditional knock-about comedy, and leavened by their own inspired zaniness, it was the first act in which Stan Laurel created a comic entity essentially his own. This is vital to consider here because Stan Laurel has always considered himself primarily a gag man. His later fame as a comedian was welcome to him, but through the years his basic comic genius has always resided in the beautifully harebrained devices he conceived—for himself, for anyone.

The Rum 'Uns from Rome described in print may seem unduly ludicrous comedy (if there can be such a thing), in this day of "line" gags and immovable comedians who arouse a portion of laughter by talking about the differences between the Democratic and Republican parties. But to heartier audiences in a hardier (and one might add, luckier) day, the act was irresistibly funny—and would be so today if there were comedians with the wild grace needed to bring it to life.

The setting is a city square in Rome of the golden age. A column containing a trap door stands stage center near a dais. A comic two-man horse enters pulling a chariot. Stan is riding the horse in full Roman regalia, brass helmet, shield, and huge ax. Dandoe is represented as riding the chariot but actually walks it across stage with his feet showing below. Dandoe mounts the dais, unrolls a parchment and says imperiously: "Gather around!"

At this point, Stan created a comic effect which was to become an essential gag in the Laurel and Hardy films. He "gathers around" literally, walking in a circle, and is stopped only by the severe look of his partner, much in the same way that Hardy later checked his idiotic sidekick when he made a similar blunder. This causes the orator and the auditor to become involved in an ax battle. Stan swings at Dandoe who escapes through the trap in the column. Suddenly a dummy head, made up like Dandoe, sticks out from behind the column and Stan buries his ax in it. The head disappears and Dandoe reappears with a duplicate ax sticking in his head, encrusted with gore. Stan removes the ax from Dandoe's head, ties great swaths of bandage around the head wound, and lacking surgical tape, pounds a nail in. Then follows an old-fashioned "cod fight" or burlesque battle whose antecedents go back to the *commedia dell' arte* and beyond. One of the men in the horse meantime comes back in a lion's skin to frighten the two who now band together to kill the intruder. This they do most effectively by feeding the beast a railroad sandwich, and they finish carrying off the moribund feline.

The Rum 'Uns from Rome ran fifteen minutes, and ran is the word. Done with lightning timing and explosive effect, the sketch came into its own in London. It gave Stan Laurel an impetus to create comedy on his own which was never to end. *Rum 'Uns* seemed doomed even with its success, however, because of a new job offer Dandoe received. Unable to turn down more money elsewhere, he quit the sketch, leaving Stan with a potential long-run hit on his hands and no one to hit over the head. He needed someone with great ability as a pantomimist and comedian, and that combination is not easily come by. Stan went into *The Wax-Works,* a sketch with and by Charles Baldwin, as an expedient and it was here that he met Ted Leo, a man who seemed to be a natural replacement for Dandoe. Stan was convinced the *Rum 'Uns* was the beginning of a new and infinitely more rewarding career for him, and with Leo working out well as his new partner, the act looked for important bookings.

One of these was at the Royal Victoria Hall, known affectionately to its many patrons in Lambeth and elsewhere as the Old Vic. Their engagement here was for a single

evening only but it carried distinction. The two partners were
not feeling particularly rum the night they went on because
they were flat broke and had no money to get their props to
the theater. They scrounged a few pennies to hire a pushcart
which they both shoved energetically down the Camberwell
Road to the Old Vic, followed by hooting urchins.

The act went beautifully that evening, and this was all the
more fortunate because Jim Reed, an old partner of Ted
Leo's, was in the audience. Reed came backstage to congrat-
ulate them and to tell them of the forming of a new act
called *Fun on the Tyrol* which was due for unveiling on the
Continent. Reed offered a job in the act to Ted who was
reluctant to do so because of his new liaison with Stan. Reed
arranged for Stan to join the group, and within the space of
a very few days, *Fun on the Tyrol,* a company of eight,
arrived for its debut in Rotterdam. Rotterdam was rainbow's
end for most of the actors: they were stony broke. Stan, like
most of his fellow artists, had not been an entire stranger to
hunger in the weeks between engagements. Rotterdam was a
new adventure and the beginning of what must surely be a
triumphal European tour. Jim Reed, as manager and director, was very fond of *Fun on the Tyrol.* For one thing he had
done the near impossible in obtaining a backer for the
troupe, a Scotland Yard detective, who had underwritten
initial expenses, and promised more. The detective, scion of a
wealthy family, had ample funds to indulge himself in a
temporary career as patron of the arts. It was a satisfied
company that arrived in Rotterdam, very satisfied, very happy and very, very poor. But payday was soon!

They were quartered in the rooms and offices of Pilcher
and Dekker, their Dutch booking agents, who owned a
saloon and restaurant in Rotterdam. Due to open a few days
after arrival, Stan and his companions were given food and
drinks on the cuff. They looked forward to their opening on
Sunday with much anticipation, and were not too dismayed
when the rain on opening night forced them to remain idle.
The Circus Variete in Rotterdam had a large wooden roof;
rain pelting down on it deafened the eardrums of anyone
sitting inside. Postponement was regrettable but in the inter-
im what better life than sitting about, eating good food and
drinking the formidable Dutch beer?

Monday it rained. Tuesday, ditto. Rain for the rest of the
week. The "on the cuff" policy was suddenly discontinued.
Reed attempted to collect some form of salary for the troupe
but he had forgotten that in his anxiety to get the booking,

he had signed a "no play, no pay" contract. Sunday again—
and suddenly the sun. *Fun on the Tyrol* opened that night
and did well. The future dawned. Monday was sheer joy. The
act had been acclaimed, the food and the beer were coming in
again in regular amounts. Tuesday—and this did not seem
possible—rain. Wednesday, rain. The contract was canceled
and Reed wired his Scotland Yard backer in London asking
him to provide transport money to Brussels where lucrative
bookings were probably waiting. In the meantime, it was the
company that waited, and food became an urgent problem.
At one point, things were so low that the liveliest members of
the company were sent out to filch bread. Stan, the most
dexterous, lurked in the corner of a bakery doorway hoping
to pluck off a few fresh loaves as the delivery man walked by
with a tray of newly baked bread on his head. As Stan
snatched a loaf, the tray jiggled slightly, and the baker's boy
turned to watch a jaunty young man walking down the street
in whistling innocence, eyes open very wide.

Hunger grew apace; the troupe literally pulled belts
tighter. Suddenly Reed obtained a week's engagement at
Liége and hope again was riding dancingly high. Liége was to
be the big beginning. No chance for a rain-out in this theater.
The first performance began. As it progressed, it played
superlatively and at furious pace. The sketch had an unusual
ending, a clever sequence featuring a stilt-walking routine.
All of the members of the troupe wore stilts of various length
and walked about the stage wearing enormous papier-mâché
heads. The tallest walker wore a comic hat which he dropped
on the stage.The smallest walker picked it up and passed it
on to the next in height, he to the next, and thus on until it
reached the tallest walker again. Stan was third from the end
in this arrangement, and on opening night he became so
overwrought with hunger pains that he fell against the man
next to him. This man fell against the next, and within a few
seconds the entire pack of cards came flipping down in a
climax of disunion and dismay.

It was the end of *Fun on the Tyrol* and almost the end of
Stan's hopes. The detective-angel arrived to pay the troupe
off, and Stan with Ted Leo was given funds to reach Brussels. Borrowing a few pounds from a friend, they reached
London and what seemed to be the conclusion of budding if
slightly frenetic careers.

"I looked like hell," Stan says. "I was tired, travel-stained,
shabby. I looked like a bum. My brother Gordon was then
manager of Prince's Theatre in London and doing very well

SAHARA TAHOE
RESORT • HOTEL • AND CASINO

A Special Invitation to

HOTEL AND MOTEL GUESTS

Enjoy the Wonderful Whirl of Excitement that is in store for you at the magnificent **SAHARA-TAHOE HOTEL & CASINO.**

Present this valuable coupon filled out in accordance with rules on back side

You will receive a special "Wonderful Whirl" assortment of **FREE ITEMS**

"Welcome to a Wonderful Whirl"

Limit: One Coupon Per Person Per Day.   Right of Refusal Reserved by Management
Program All or In Part at Option of Sahara-Tahoe Management

AUTHORIZED PROPERTY STAMP

GOOD THIS DATE ONLY

Hyatt Lodge

(Must be stamped; handwritten dating is not acceptable)

Room Number 118

Limit: One Coupon Per Person Per Day
Right of Refusal Reserved by Management

This special bonus offer is made only to guests
of Lake Tahoe area hotels and motels.
Employees of participating properties are not
eligible.

for himself. He had a beautiful flat in High Holborn, and I walked all the way there from Waterloo Station without a penny in my pockets. He wasn't there so I walked over to the theater to see him. I saw him just as I reached the outside of the theater. He had on a high hat and a cutaway. He looked about as different from me as it's possible to get, so I waited until he had finished talking with some friends before I approached him. I didn't want to have him recognize me as his brother in front of people. He saw me and took me up to the office and read me a friendly lecture. 'Stan,' he said, 'why do you want to be a comic? You'll never make any money, let alone a name for yourself.' And just at that moment, I was pretty sure he was right."

Gordon gave him a job as a super in Dion Boucicault's *Ben Machree* then playing at the Prince's. During this period he took on a variety of odd jobs not the least prepossessing of which was one as a part-time script typist.

Shortly before this, *A Night in an English Music Hall* had returned from its extended tour of the States. Walking in Leicester Square one afternoon, Stan met Alf Reeves, Karno's manager for the American tour. Alf, the brother of Billy Reeves, the original Drunk in the act, was arranging for a new American tour, and he offered Stan his old job. The salary was raised to a munificent $30 a week, $5 over the old salary, and Stan was now to be understudy to Chaplin who had fallen full-time heir to the role of The Drunk. The company sailed within a week and began a tour on the Sullivan-Considine circuit opening at the Empress Theatre, Cincinnati. Stan expected the tour to be merely a pleasant interval in his life before he returned to London and began once more the essential task of making *The Rum 'Uns from Rome* the best turn on the halls. Actually, he would not return until 1932 when he and Oliver Hardy received a tumultuous welcome the equal of any ever given any entertainers in the history of Great Britain.

The second tour of *A Night in an English Music Hall* was successful with one qualification. Charlie Chaplin left the company in that year, 1913. For some months before in far-off Hollywood, Mack Sennett had been in need of a leading comedian. His top-line comic, Ford Sterling, was becoming restless, feeling that he needed the satisfaction of more money and greater opportunities than the Sennett lot offered him. Sennett and Mabel Normand had seen the Karno company in New York and the antics of The Drunk persisted in their memory. They now offered Chaplin $125 a week, a considerable jump over his weekly $75 stipend from Karno. Chaplin reported to Sennett in late 1913. *A Night in an English Music Hall* lasted a month more.

Various theaters refused to take the company if it did not include Chaplin as The Drunk. Stan was considered too young for the part, although he had played it as a substitute. Karno, in desperation, laid the company off for three weeks while he went back to get Dan Raynor, a new lead comedian, from England. Raynor, like the others, failed "to follow" Chaplin, and the company closed for good.

In the search for something to occupy him, Stan felt the old desire to do his own act bubbling up. His best friends in the company were Edgar Hurley and his wife; the three talked at length and combined to become *The Three Comiques*, a burglar sketch. This slight skit which played its first date on the "small time" around Chicago is in essence an embryonic, early Laurel and Hardy one-reeler. Stan and Edgar are two noisy and clumsy burglars who enter an apartment in search of a safe. They are interrupted by the maid. She is mollified by their explanation that they are icemen. One of the burglars begins a flirtation with her while his confederate continues his search for loot. In attempting to open the safe, the second comic lights a hand bomb which begins to sputter unexpectedly. Then follows the old routine of passing the bomb back and forth between each other in frenzy until one of them throws it out the window. Explosion. Policeman enters in rage and black-powdered face and arrests them. Blackout.

While playing this act in Cleveland, Kalma, an illusionist on the bill, suggested that they try to make the big time, and to that end he introduced *The Three Comiques* to his agents, Claude and Gordon Bostock. The Bostocks eventually wired them in Pittsburgh announcing their promotion to the two-a-day on the Keith circuit opening in Jersey City. Changing their name to *Hurley, Stan and Wren*, the act opened in Jersey City, and with suggested changes from the Bostocks, they were now prepared to assault the highest pinnacle of American vaudeville—the Orpheum circuit.

The suggested changes were vital ones. Taking their name from the Sennett company, *Hurley, Stan and Wren* became *The Keystone Trio*. Stan did an imitation of Chaplin, Hurley became Chester Conklin, and Wren was Mabel Normand. Stan was the first of a long line of vaudeville comedians to imitate Chaplin. There was, however, an important difference. He not only knew Chaplin and his mannerisms well from the Karno days, but he brought to the imitation a talent for mime that was almost as great as Chaplin's. *The Keystone Trio* opened at the Columbia Theatre in New York on a show date for a group of big agents. This was to be their proving ground; they would now either get into the big time for good or slide right back to the minor circuits.

The Columbia Theatre date was triumphant. The agents were excited and pleased. "Even if I have to say it myself," Stan says, "we were a bloody sensation." *The Keystone Trio* had made the long climb into the Orpheum circuit, and there was not much doubt about new and happier times ahead.

But Stan had forgotten one thing. Edgar Hurley, a good but not overly talented comedian, like Bottom, wanted to play the lion, too. Annoyed by the personal success of Stan's Chaplin, he demanded the right to play the part on occasion. He did it—once—in New York at Proctor's Fifth Avenue Theatre. That day the act, in Stan's words, "died a dog's death." Most of the laughs that had always greeted the Laurel Chaplin were missing when Hurley tried his hand at this performance. At one point in the act Stan-as-Chaplin invariably received a large and extended laugh followed by great applause. Hurley worked hard to duplicate this laugh and, failing to get the strong reaction at this moment, walked down to the footlights and sarcastically started to lead his own applause. A few seconds later, he took the audience into his confidence with the remark that Stan always wanted to be the funny man in the act, and what did they think about that? Luckily, Bostock was in the audience and he warned Hurley that the act could not survive under such conditions. *The Keystone Trio* reached Proctor's Theatre in Newark and expired in an atmosphere of hearty recrimination.

It was another almost unendurable blow to Stan. The act, as originally conceived, was one of the most brilliant ever to play American vaudeville circuits—the agents had told him this—and yet, in ultimate analysis, the act's demise was a disguised blessing. Stan Laurel might have gone on to become the best permanent imitator of Charlie Chaplin, thereby forcing his own superb wit and great mimetic ability into a form outside its own.

What to do but be up again and doing with another act? Forming one under his own name, *The Stan Jefferson Trio* began the circuit tours. Again, with a burglar theme like *The Three Comiques,* the new trio started up the uneasy road to vaudeville success. In the continually changing process of improving the act, Stan began to incorporate songs and dances, and within a few months the old act had been changed to a completely new entity to which he wished to give a new name.

"Just about this time," he says, "I started thinking of a new name for myself. When I first started in show business, I used my full name, Stanley Jefferson. This I broke down to Stan Jefferson. Then one day, quite by accident, I happened to notice that my name had thirteen letters in it. I figured the superstition department might be the cause so I decided to make a change. Funny—I don't know why I picked Laurel. Honestly can't remember. Just sounded good, I guess. However, my hunch was right! Things started to get better right away, and after I got known in pictures, I had my name legalized."

With a name and a new act, Stan played up and down and around the country for two years. His principal partner in the act was a young Australian singer and dancer who assumed his new name both for reasons of euphony and marquee-space economy. *Stan and Mae Laurel* proved to be a staple bit of fare for vaudeville fans all over the country during this period. Unlike many other acts on the principal circuits, it had the advantage of having a first-class gag-man as its director. Stan kept adding gags, taking them out, embellishing others—continually at work.

Early in 1917, Stan was booked into the Hippodrome, Los Angeles. The house was owned by Adolph Ramish, a very wealthy and a very unpretentious man. Stan noticed that a pleasant-looking, short, chubby individual with a look of shabby gentility usually watched the act from the wings. He had always thought him to be the janitor, and after receiving a call to see the boss, he was considerably baffled to meet the less-than-resplendent Mr. Ramish in his office.

"I've been watching you from the wings," said Ramish.

"I know," Stan said. "Hope you like us."

"I like you all right. It's my personal opinion that you're funnier than Chaplin. Would you like to make some pictures?"

"Pictures? Why, I—when?"

"Now," answered Ramish. "I'll rent a studio and crew and with your ideas we can make some really funny two-reelers. How about it?"

Stan was eager to try but recalled that he had eight weeks to go on his present contract on the circuit and could not afford to knock off work and wait for studio arrangements to be completed. Ramish assured him that he would pay him $75 a week until the films were under way, and with a handshake as a new contract, the plans for the first Stan Laurel film went forward.

Ramish hired Bobby Williamson to direct the first film. Williamson, himself a former comic, had been directing one-reel comedies in Florida featuring, among others, another up-and-coming young man named Oliver Hardy. Stan and Williamson got together to talk over a plot and came up with a simple story of a man escaping from an insane asylum, attired in a business suit but wearing a Napoleon hat. Titled *Nuts in May,* this two-reeler film was shot at a small studio in Royle Heights, Los Angeles. Ramish previewed the film at the Hippodrome and invited Charlie Chaplin and Carl Laemmle to see it.

Fortunately, the film was unusually funny.

It is difficult, perhaps, for most film-goers to think of Stan Laurel as anything other than a dim-witted clown, slow, sauntering casually through incredible situations and given only to violent action after considerable external stimuli. To picture him as a freewheeling, ebullient comedian in the Chaplin tradition is not easy, and yet that is precisely what he was. His early films, made years before he met Hardy, reveal him to be a spare, rather handsome young man, given to much vigorous movement and unusually swift-paced panto-mimic action. The resemblances to the early Chaplin are unmistakable. This was not only due to the circumstance that Stan had but shortly before imitated Chaplin in vaudeville, nor was it because he had understudied Chaplin in the Karno days. It was because Chaplin and Laurel share one mag-nificent heritage—the English music hall. They had early on learned the hard lesson of pantomime. A music hall artist frequently was forced to play the halls of Europe for economic reasons, and in this way, it became necessary for him not to depend on language. Additionally, the halls had through long years developed a great tradition of utter non-sense. It is a British characteristic in humor to do nonsense gravely.

This was the kind of performance Stan Laurel gave in *Nuts in May,* his first film, and as Charlie Chaplin sat in the Hippodrome watching it, he knew that here was a man of his own talents—a man, true, who had not yet found his form, but a man destined to be a film comedian, and a very great one.

Stan and Charlie had dinner after the film. Chaplin told

Stan that he was tired of Mutual, his current studio, and had been planning a studio of his own. He had conceived of a project which he felt sure would be financially and artistically successful. In addition to filming his own comedies, he wanted to form another stock company of screen comedians to produce a separate series of films. This company would be semiautonomous and would rent facilities at the Chaplin studios. Would Stan like to be a part of this project? Stan would and hoped he could. Stan told Ramish the following day that the project was in the offing, but that he would await Ramish's pleasure on any future move because he felt a deep obligation to the amiable theater owner. Ramish suggested that while they were waiting for Chaplin's next move, a one-reeler might be made. The following day, Carl Laemmle called and suggested that if *Nuts in May* was typical of the Laurel talent, he would do well working for Universal. Stan said that he would not do anything without Ramish's approval; the latter pointed out that nothing should be done until Chaplin had declared rather stronger intentions.

Stan made a real effort to discover Chaplin's plans. He finally reached him at Levy's, a restaurant, and sent a note to him asking if they might get together. Chaplin sent back word of the traditional don't-call-me-I'll-call-you nature. Chaplin never called.

In later years, Stan wondered idly at times what might have happened if Chaplin had called. Such speculations, of course, are endless. It is more than probable that there would have been no Laurel and Hardy. Perhaps Stan would have continued in his own pattern, the volatile, music hall-attuned mime not unlike the early Chaplin character. Perhaps he might have gone on to act as a gag man or director for Chaplin. In retrospect, Stan admits, things went rather well anyway.

Laemmle wanted an answer, and in a few weeks Ramish made a one-year deal for Stan with Universal Studios. On the Universal lot, in keeping with the current Hollywood custom of assuming a unique character identification, Stan became "Hickory Hiram." Hiram was a rustic and not a terribly funny one. "I can't remember any of the Hickory Hiram films," Stan admits. "I never saw rushes during shooting or even on completion. It is my personal recollection that they were released at all the first-run comfort stations." Jealousy among other Universal comedians complicated his stay there; moreover, the studio was going through a period of reorganization. After three or four Hirams, Laemmle made a sweeping change in studio procedures and canceled all contracts. Stan again was a free agent in the most literal sense, and there faced him a single alternative. Vaudeville. Back to the two—or three—or four a day. This was a *hell* of a way to make a living.

Chapter II

MR. HARDY

Hull, England
(On tour)
21 November 1953

Dear Jack:

I think the idea of a book is a very good one, and I shall do everything in my power to help you, of course. I especially like the idea that it will be about our way of making the pictures, rather than about our lives. When we return to Birmingham, you can spend all the time you like interviewing us together or separately, as you like. Probably I can be of more help to you in that department than Babe. He usually doesn't care to talk too much about the making of the pictures. . . .

Stan

3 August 1958

Dear Prof. McCabe:

Thank you very much for your recent letter . . . I have been tracking down all the information I can get at, contacting a lot of people who knew Babe in the old days, checking through old scrapbooks and the like . . . In regard to the printing of your interview with Babe in Birmingham, I am not at this point in favor of it. I hope I am not throwing a monkey wrench into things for you, but I am very definitely opposed to such a method of presentation. . . .

Yours sincerely,
Lucille Hardy

31 October 1958

Dear Prof. McCabe:

Here at last some material for you. . . . Regarding your interview with Babe in Birmingham which you would like to print . . . it is such a true picture of Babe's character, such a genuine revelation of several very important facets of his nature—just so typically Babe—that anyone who knew him well would recognize these things immediately after reading it. Perhaps that is the very reason I resented it and mentally rejected it on first reading. Analyzing it and myself now after a passage of time—and reading it and rereading it—I can see that, being so close to the picture and so emotionally involved, it hit with quite a shock. I could hear and see him: each inflection of the voice, his facial mannerisms—and even anticipate his thought processes. That's what you can do when you have loved and understood a person for so many years. It brought everything back too vividly and I suspect that, selfishly, I temporarily resented sharing it with anyone else . . . so, it is up to you as to whether you want it printed or not. Handle it as you like in order to make for the best and most interesting treatment and presentation. . . .

Yours sincerely,
Lucille Hardy

Transcript of interview,
Birmingham, England. January 1954.

Query: Mr. Hardy, the purpose of all this is to find out what I can about your background in relationship to comedy.

Hardy: I see.

Query: The way the book has been set out, your life story will occupy all of the second chapter—that is, your life until the time you teamed up with Stan. What I'd like to know principally about you during your early years—outside of the normally interesting biographical details—is how and why you came to be a comedian, the things that make you laugh—and so on.

Hardy: Well, that won't take long.

Query: Pardon?

Hardy: That won't take long.

Query: In what sense?

Hardy: What I said. It won't take long. I hate to be discouraging, but there's very little to write about me.

Query: You don't think I can even get an entire chapter out of you?

Hardy: You can try, but I warn you: there's very little to say. Stan can fill you in on all the comedy stuff done in the pictures—and as for my life, it wasn't very exciting and I didn't do very much outside of doing a lot of gags before a camera and play golf the rest of the time.

Query: We'll get what we can. Anyway, where were you born? And when?

Hardy: Harlem, Georgia. January 18, 1892.

Query: And your family?

Hardy: My father, Oliver Hardy, was a lawyer and he died when I was quite young. He was of English stock and one of his ancestors was close to Admiral Nelson. You may remember that when Nelson was dying on the deck of his ship, one of his last words were, "Kiss me, Hardy" to his aide-de-camp. I can trace my ancestry directly back to that Hardy. My mother's name was Emily Norvell and she was of Scottish descent. My full name is Oliver Norvell Hardy.

Query: I notice that at various times in the pictures, you use your full name. Is there a reason for that?

Hardy: I use it in full sometimes when I want to sound very impressive. There's something about a three-barreled name that sounds impressive, and besides I think my name *does* sound impressive. I like the sound of it—and one thing I want to emphasize: I never use my name to make fun of it. I'm proud of my name—all of it.

Query: Any one in your family come from show business?

Hardy: Not one. I came from a family of three boys and two girls. Neither they, my folks, or as far as I know anyone who came before us, had anything to do with show business. But our entire family loved music and the theater. We were very fond of singing; I became a boy tenor when I was quite young and my mother always encouraged my desire to sing.

Query: What was your boyhood like?

Hardy: Very ordinary. As a boy, I lived in Madison, Georgia, where my mother ran a hotel. Nothing very exciting about that except that as a child I got into a habit that I still have.

Query: And that is?

Hardy: Lobby watching.

Query: You sit in the lobby—

Hardy: I sit in the lobby and I watch people. I like to watch people. Once in a while someone will ask me where Stan and I dreamed up the characters we play in the movies. They seem to think that these two fellows aren't like anybody else. I know they're *dumber* than anyone else, but there are plenty of Laurels and Hardys in the world. Whenever I travel, I still am in the habit of sitting in the lobby and watching the people walk by—and I tell you I see many Laurels and Hardys. I used to see them in my mother's hotel when I was a kid: the dumb, dumb guy who never has anything bad happen to him—and the smart, smart guy who's dumber than the dumb guy only he doesn't know it.

Query: What was your education?

Hardy: I went to school at Georgia Military College, which was a government supervised military academy. Oh, I forgot to tell you that when I was eight years old, I joined Coburn's Minstrels for a while. We were on tour all over the South but I was really too young for that life so I came back home.

Query: What did you do in the minstrel show?

Hardy: I was a boy soprano. Had two big hit songs, "Silver Threads Among the Gold" and "When You and I Were Young, Maggie."

Query: Did you keep up with your music?

Hardy: Yes. Some years later my mother sent me to the Atlanta Conservatory of Music where I studied under Adolph Dahm Peterson, one of the best musicians in the South. I'm going to brag here a bit. Everyone thought I was quite remarkable because I could hit high C.

Query: Did you intend to become a professional singer?

Hardy: I suppose it was always in the back of my mind but I didn't give it much conscious thought. It appears to me as if I never really made up my mind to do anything very definite. I did want to be a lawyer for a while and studied for a bit at the University of Georgia, but I gave that up.

Query: How did you get into show business?

Hardy: Funny thing, but I guess I actually got into show business from the real business end. My mother moved to Milledgeville, Georgia, from Madison, and somewhere around 1910, I opened the first movie theater ever to be built in town. I'm pretty sure it was 1910 because I remember running the results of the Johnson-Jeffries fight on a slide one day.

Query: Did running a film house give you your first interest in films and film-making?

Hardy: Yes. I saw some of the comedies that were being made and I thought to myself that I could be as good—or maybe as *bad*—as some of those boys. So in 1913, I gave up the movie theater and went on to Jacksonville, Florida. I started to work for Lubin Motion Pictures. I made $5 a day—with three days' work a week guaranteed. In those days Lubin made what was called "split-reel" work; they would make a thousand-foot reel and put two five-hundred-foot comedies on it.

Query: Then you were basically a comedian from the beginning?

Hardy: Yes. I always played a "heavy"—you know, the

villain—and I usually appeared in comedies. Once in a while, I've played it straight but not usually. I guess my weight just automatically made me a heavy—which is a hell of a joke —but perfectly true.

Query: Are you what one might call naturally heavy? Have you ever tried to reduce at any time in your life?

Hardy: Well, the doctors tell me that I should try to start cutting down now because I'm over 300 pounds and that isn't good for the heart. But, no, I never really tried to cut down and, of course, after Stan and I got known as fat and skinny it just wasn't smart to cut down on my weight. But for many years there when we did our pictures, I wasn't really fat. I've always been big; I'm big-boned. Every one in my family was big.

Query: Was there anything special about your work at Lubin that had an influence on your later work with Stan?

Hardy: Yes, there was one picture I made in 1915 that seemed to have some kind of tie-in with the pictures I made with Stan later. The picture was called *The Paperhanger's Helper*. Now, I hadn't met Stan at this time and I wouldn't for some years to come. And yet this picture, in a way, was like a Laurel and Hardy comedy. I made the picture with Bobby Ray, who was a slight man, on the short side. Didn't look like Stan but he was an opposite to me. I'll tell you what I can remember about the plot. We were paperhangers; I was the boss, Bobby was my helper. I was always giving him orders and he was always getting the short end of the stick. I remember we were walking up a hill. He was pulling our cart loaded with wallpaper. I wasn't doing my work naturally. We get up to the top and I tell him we're on the wrong street. He lets the wagon fly back down the hill and then it gets mixed up with a wagon that has a lot of circus posters on it. We reclaim our wagon and go over to the job we're working on which is a hospital. So, as you can imagine, the rest of the picture (it was a two-reeler) is full of stuff about getting circus billboards mixed up with the regular paper and all that. Bobby always played the fall guy; I was the wise guy just as I am in Laurel and Hardy, only in Laurel and Hardy, *I* always am the fall guy. I think of that picture once in a while as being the start of the Laurel and Hardy idea as far as I was concerned.

Query: Mr. Hardy—

Hardy: Babe. Please call me Babe.

Query: Where did you get the nickname of Babe?

Hardy: In Florida, when I was working for Lubin. We

used to get our hair cut at an Italian barber's who had a shop right near our studio. He had a thick foreign accent and he was also a boy who liked boys. Well, he took a great fancy to me and every time after he'd finish shaving me, he'd rub powder into my face and pat my cheeks and say, "Nice-a bab-ee. Nice-a bab-ee." The gang always used to kid me about it and after a while they started to call me "Baby" and then it was cut down to "Babe"—and I've been Babe Hardy ever since.

Query: How long were you with Lubin?

Hardy: About three years. I gradually worked up to star comic. Then I went to New York for a while and did some free-lance work in various film companies. Can't remember much about that now. Then, in 1917 I went back to Jacksonville and did some cabaret work as a singer. And I also did some pictures for Vim Comedies in Jacksonville. They were making one-reelers there at the time. A few months later, I went back to New York and I worked as the heavy in the Billy West comedies. He was very popular at the time.

Query: He was a Chaplin imitator, wasn't he?

Hardy: That's right. And I did almost all the heavies opposite him, the way Swain and Campbell did for Chaplin. I put on a heavy beard and wore heavy eyebrows. Then when Billy West folded in December 1918, I went to California.

Query: For whom did you work?

Hardy: I started to work for Vitagraph, and then I did heavies with Jimmy Aubrey who was making two-reelers then. I also worked with Earl Williams—and, oh, a lot of others. Then, I started with Larry Semon.

Query: And heavies again.

Hardy: What else?

Query: You were working with him in the days when he was at the top, weren't you?

Hardy: Yes. No one was bigger than Larry when he was on top. He was a good comedian—a very good acrobatic comedian—and he always knew a good gag when he saw one. He used to have a little black book that he'd keep in his back trouser pocket. That little book was worth thousands and thousands of dollars because he always kept all his comedy ideas in it. I never saw anyone work harder at making a gag work out, except maybe Stan.

Query: Haven't you been interested in creating gags?

Hardy: No. Not that I didn't appreciate a good gag, mind you. I like to get a good reaction just the way any comedian does, but I have never really worked hard in the creation department. After all, just *doing* the gags is hard enough work especially if you've taken as many falls and been dumped in as many mudholes as I have. I think I've earned my money.

Query: There are millions of people all over the world who'll agree with you. But I'm interested to know if there was ever any kind of influence over you in the creation of the particular character you play with Stan. The character was not just created on the spot, was it?

Hardy: No, the character grew—sort of gradually. I had always worn a derby from my early days in Florida, but the Ollie Hardy character was partly based on "Helpful Henry." "Helpful Henry" was a cartoon character in Georgia newspapers when I was a boy. He was always trying to be helpful but he was always making a mess of things. He was very big and fussy and important but underneath it all, he was a very nice guy. That's very much like the character I play.

Query: Why did you and Stan use your own names in pictures? Don't you feel sort of strange having your own name identified with that of a big nitwit?

Hardy: In the early days of comedy, the studio frequently owned the character name, like "Lonesome Luke" or "Hickory Hiram" or some such and the comedian could be fired but he couldn't take his character name with him. So we just kept our own names. Couldn't steal *those* from us. And, no, I don't mind being identified with the nitwit. After all, he is a very nice person underneath.

Query: I notice that in the films both you and Stan show great respect for each other when you are introducing yourselves.

Hardy: That's right. Whenever I introduce him, it's always, "I'd like you to meet my friend, Mr. Laurel" and vice versa. These two fellows we created, they are nice, very nice people. They never get anywhere because they are both so very dumb but they don't *know* that they're dumb. One of the reasons why people like us, I guess, is because they feel so superior to us. Even an eight-year-old kid can feel superior to us, and that makes him laugh. But to get back to that "Mr. Laurel" and "Mr. Hardy" thing. These two fellows have as much right to exist as anybody on earth and they have just as much right to be called "Mr." In fact, some of the people they call "Mister" nowadays ... Well, Stan and Ollie are real people and they are good people. So, I don't feel bad that people connect me with a very dumb guy. In my opinion, he is also a very nice guy—and there are a lot of him around.

Query: You have, of course, some traces left of your Southern accent. And, also, would it be right to say that in the pictures you still use what may be described as Southern manners—the sort of courtly or gallant way of addressing women and introducing men, and so on?

Hardy: Yes, I guess you'd call it Southern manners. That's the way I was brought up. I was taught to be courteous at whatever cost to myself, and so in the pictures, I always am very mannerly to people because I think that's the way one should be all the time. Of course, I exaggerate for comic effect but I still mean it. It's basically the way I feel.

Query: I don't quite know how to put this but for a big man, you move very easily and gracefully. Is there some special reason for this?

Hardy: I always try to walk lightly. I don't like to see heavy men lurching all over the place; there's no real need for it. I've always loved to dance and I suppose that's why I've learned how to walk easily.

Query: Well, I guess that's it, Babe. I think I've got all the essential information I need—but one final question. You've had a very full life and career. What was the best part of it—or the finest thing that happened to you?

Hardy: I've had so many nice things happen to me and I've had so much fun that it's sort of hard to sort out. But I guess you'd call my best moment this one. When I was a boy, my mother would occasionally go to fortunetellers and one day she went to visit a lady in Decatur, Georgia. This lady told Mama that one day her son's name would be known all over the world. It's nice to know that she saw that prophecy come true.

31 October 1958

Dear Jack:

I think probably the best arrangement in trying to give you the information you think the public would like to have about Babe is for you to send along your questions to me, and I'll answer as fully as I can. I do so want people to know Babe as he really was. I want to show the side of him the public never knew—the side that I, as his wife, would want the world to know.

First, I think I'll give you just a few general things about him and his background, and then I'll wait for your letters.

He really did have a beautiful singing voice. As the youngest of five children, he was encouraged by everyone in the family, including his mother who operated the Baldwin Hotel

in Milledgeville, Georgia, after the death of her husband. She
loved to hear him sing, and he sang because he enjoyed it
tremendously. Many theatrical people stayed at his mother's
hotel—performers in tent shows, Chautauquas and the like—
and they fascinated Babe. They told so many fascinating
stories that Babe ran away from home at the age of eight to
join Coburn's Minstrels! There's no doubt that many of these
stories told to him were elaborations of the truth, and after a
while the "glamor" of the theater began to wear off. His
mother knew where he was, of course; she corresponded with
Mr. Coburn who ran the Minstrels (this was Charles Coburn—
not *the* Charles Coburn—but a distant cousin), and Mr.
Coburn assured Mrs. Hardy that he would keep a paternal
eye on young Norvell—Babe was always known as Norvell as
a youngster. Well, Mrs. Hardy figured that he would eventually get show business out of his blood and come home one
day. He did come home, but despite all the loneliness and
lack of family love on the road, he could not get rid of his
love of the theater.

. . . For the next few years, he was very faithful in his
home duties. He would help out at the hotel and all in all was
a very obedient son, but once again he started to hang out
with the performers, running errands for them in order to get
money to see the "big" shows in Atlanta, and just generally
getting himself more and more involved with show people
. . . Sometimes he would have just enough money to get to
Atlanta and buy a ticket in the top gallery without having a
penny to come home on, but he saw the show—and that was
the important thing . . . He started to neglect school so his
mother sent him away to boarding school in order to force
his attention on his studies, but he couldn't stand it. . . . He
ran away to Atlanta, and although he didn't know it, it was
the day of the big race riot, April 17, 1906. He found refuge
in the railroad station, his clothes all caked with red mud,
and the very kindly stationmaster helped him clean up and
also telephoned Mrs. Hardy. She lost no time in coming after
him, but he refused to go back to school.

So she let him stay in Atlanta to study voice. As far as she
was concerned, he was now happy, doing just what he
wanted. A few weeks later, however, when she came back to
Atlanta to check up on things, she found out that he hadn't
been attending his music classes for weeks. Professor Peterson, his instructor, said: "The young man has a beautiful
voice—but no damned ambish!" She found Babe in a movie
house singing to illustrated slides at a salary of 50¢ a day. He

was sent back to school but was allowed to sing on Saturdays and holidays. . . .

He had a very happy family life despite the loss of his father. His oldest sister, Mrs. Elizabeth Sage, is still living in Atlanta, and in a letter received from her, she tells about that. She said: "Norvell was the baby of the family and, of course, he was just adored by all of us as the sweetest baby who ever lived. He was really a beautiful boy, had such a handsome face. In fact, I think he was handsome all of his life even if he was heavy. He did use to eat a lot as a boy, he was awfully fond of his food. I can remember that he weighed 250 pounds at the age of fourteen. That was when he was sent away to military school at Milledgeville. He didn't like it there because all the boys used to make jokes about fat boys and he didn't like it one little bit. But even at that, he had the sweetest disposition, and he always was such a sportsman about everything. He could stand up to a lot of kidding and he could hand out the kidding, too. And he had a mind of his own. I can remember a few times that when he was at military school during the drill period, he would just get so tired that he would simply lie down flat on the ground and not budge an inch. They just couldn't move him! He was tired and that was that! The headmaster at the academy (he was a great friend of Mother's) used to call him 'the funniest boy in the world.' At commencement exercises one year, the undergraduates put on a 'Who Killed Cock Robin?' skit. At the climax of the skit, the chorus came out singing 'Who Killed Cock Robin?' Norvell came out in costume and sang in his glorious tenor voice 'I killed Cock Robin! I tolled the bell because I could pull the rope. *I am the bull!*' And, there he was, so big and with such a lovely voice that it just broke up the proceedings right then and there. Everybody just leaned back and howled. He was such a funny thing and such a dear thing. Even at that time he displayed a wonderful stage presence and personality.

"He could get angry, though. He would take kidding about his size but only up to a certain point. Back home he was always asked to umpire the local baseball games because of the good show he put on. There used to be a saying around town that they'd close the banks to see Norvell umpire. Well, sometimes he would make some decisions that weren't popular with the crowd and the crowd would start calling him Fatty and Fats, and Norvell would just stomp off and threaten to go home if the crowd kept on. They never let him go. He was the life of the town.

"As I said, he always ate a lot. Once he ran away from military school because he said they didn't feed him enough. He refused to go back until his mother had made him *twenty* baking powder biscuits which he ate at one sitting! I think that maybe he always ate so much because he missed the father he lost when he was ten.

"And yet he was always the happiest thing when folks were around to be entertained. I remember once he was sent off to a mountain school run by close family friends. He was the life of the party there, too. Once while camping out, he climbed a tree while all the other students were around down below, and he sang: 'Lawd, if you don't help me, don't help that bear!' They just howled. So, it was no surprise when he went into show business. He thought once of going into law but when he talked to the family about it, they just all said: 'Why, Norvell, you're just a big fat baby. How'd you ever win a law suit?' And that decided it. It was so natural for him to be a comedian. It was the most natural thing in the world. He was so funny . . . and he was so sweet."

And that's what Babe's sister remembers best about him. But to get back to the years when he was at home. . . . One summer . . . Babe's older brother was killed in a swimming accident. Babe and a friend pulled him from the water, and he decided then that he should be of more help to his mother so he made up his mind to become a lawyer and buckle down to studying . . . but that was short-lived. He was back to singing again . . . He joined a minstrel show as an end man. (He had a great admiration for Lew Dockstader and tried to pattern his style on his.) In 1910, he opened the first movie house in Milledgeville as he told you in his interview. As you can imagine, this kept him busy but one day, in 1913, he heard of some film activity in Jacksonville, Florida. He went there, got a job singing in a cabaret at night and spent his days hunting for work in the studios. Most of the movies made those days were shot outdoors so it wasn't difficult for him to follow various companies about, getting acquainted with the cast and crew. It's there that he made his first movie.

Sincerely,
Lucille

14 November 1958

Dear Lucille:
. . . Any details about his first films will be appreciated.

Did he do comedy, and was this under his own name? Did he engage in any active military service during World War I?

Sincerely,
Jack

18 November 1958

Dear Jack:

He did everything when once he actually got into the pictures. He wasn't working, just hanging around watching the Lubin company work one day when suddenly they needed a fat boy for a comedy sequence. He was Johnny-on-the-spot and he was hired at $5 a day, three days a week guarantee. But he came to work every day whether he was paid or not just to watch, watch, watch and learn. He would lug film and props from one set-up to another. He helped the grips, the painters, the carpenters, everybody.

Lubin later became Vim Comedies and Babe worked for both organizations. He started with bits, then comedy-bits, comedy-support, stooge, comedy-characterizations and sometimes straight heavy. (The villains in those days were always called "heavies." Their trademark was usually *heavy* eyebrows and mustache make-up.) Production then was a far cry from what it is today. They seldom had a script to start with—just an idea. Someone might suggest that it looked like a good day for fishing or for digging clams and off they would go to a spot along the St. Johns River or the beach, taking along all the necessary equipment, wardrobe, etc., to see what would "develop." And sure enough something always did. Everybody helped everybody in those days. The cast helped the crew when making set-ups and the crew helped the cast—many times acting as background extras when needed. Babe, for instance, many times during filming, worked in turn as script clerk, assistant cameraman, assistant director, and once in a while during emergencies even became the director. So, he learned the motion picture business from the ground up, although he always preferred to be in front of the camera.

He remained with Lubin and Vim (except for a brief period in New York in 1917) until about mid-1918. As he told you, it was in Florida that he acquired the nickname of "Babe" and he was even billed as such in his early pictures. A few years later, feeling he wasn't progressing as fast as he'd like, he consulted a numerologist who advised him to change his name. He had always liked his father's name, Oliver Hardy, so he changed his own from Norvell Hardy to Oliver

Norvell Hardy legally, using Oliver Hardy for billing. The studio didn't approve at first because he had established himself as "Babe" Hardy, but eventually they compromised on Oliver "Babe" Hardy. It was not until after he went to Hollywood that he was able to drop the "Babe," and, as history records, his career did zoom from then on. The nickname "Babe," however, was to stay with him the remainder of his life as a term of affection from his family and friends. . . . Also in Jacksonville, he joined the Masons, Solomon Order Lodge No. 20, F.A.M. and became a Master Mason, an affiliation of which he was very proud all his life. He tried to live up to Masonic ideals at all times, and he was extremely happy and grateful to be made a life member in the Solomon Lodge in October 1948.

I mentioned the fact that he paid a brief visit to New York in early 1917. He was curious about the big city, so he decided to give it a try. It was tougher going than in Florida, though, and he didn't like the cold or the bigness of the city. He did a few pictures with Jimmy Aubrey and made other free-lance films while trying to keep up with his singing. His singing career wasn't going so well because he found the competition much tougher than in Florida, and, all in all, he was not enchanted with New York. The final blow came when we entered the war in April 1917. Babe was working at one of the studios on the New Jersey side the day war came, and he headed for the nearest recruiting office fired with enthusiasm and genuine patriotic feeling. He walked in and announced his intention to enlist. The officer in charge didn't even answer. He gaped at Babe for a moment, looked him up and down and yelled into another office, "Hey, Sarge, come look at what wants to enlist!" The sergeant came out, looked, and the two doubled up with laughter. This was followed by a number of remarks intended to be funny, but they were anything but funny to Babe. He was terribly hurt and embarrassed—and this finished him with New York. He completed the job he was doing and then went back to Vim in Florida and a night job at the Burbidge Hotel cabaret there. He did go back to New York in 1918 for a while to work as the heavy in the Billy West comedies, and this time he was more kindly disposed toward the town, but he didn't stay long. He had been hearing of the film boom in California, and he headed there, late in 1918. He found that most of his friends in Jacksonville had gone West too. So he went out and worked for a great number of people: Billy West, Earl

Williams at Vitagraph, L-KO Studios, Jimmy Aubrey, Larry
Semon, William Fox, and of course, ultimately, Hal Roach
. . .

Sincerely,
Lucille

2 December 1958
Dear Lucille:
I think that at this point I'd like to know the details of
your meeting with Babe and although I naturally don't want
you to reveal anything that you'd consider purely personal,
yet I hope you can tell me the reasons why you loved him. I
think this would help us to know more about him . . .

Sincerely,
Jack

8 December 1958
Dear Jack:
In July 1939 I was hired by Boris Morros as script clerk
on the boys' picture *The Flying Deuces*. I had a run-in with
Babe the first day of shooting, only a few hours after meeting
him. The master scene had been shot and the camera had
moved in for an individual shot of Babe. His hat, which had
been off in the master scene, was on. He wasn't holding his
gloves and cane as he had been doing in the previous scene
so I started to tell him this just before the shooting began.
(This is a part of keeping everything in the film in continuity
and was an essential part of my job.) In a very gentlemanly
way and with an almost courtly gesture, he stopped me by
saying, "I know how it was, my dear. Don't you worry. *I'll*
take care of everything." I was so humiliated that I was
speechless. My face turned red as a beet and I walked away
thinking that somebody as pompous and conceited as that
was just bound to mess everything up.

But the minute the camera turned, I saw how wrong I
was. He became the character he had been portraying. The
dialogue, the mannerisms, every little gesture was flawless
and matched the master scene perfectly. This always amazed
me over the years—his perfection with lines and gestures.
After we had been married, I learned one reason why he always
knew so well what he was doing; he would always rehearse
his lines for the next day as soon as he got home. We would
go through them together (he learned lines quickly) and
then, just before bed, he would go through them again. Many
actors in pictures tend to study their lines on the set in the

morning with the thought, particularly in comedy—or as sometimes happens, with the *excuse*—that the dialogue would probably be changed. Not Babe. Even when he *knew* the dialogue was going to be changed, he would study the scene closely to get the feel.

But getting back to *The Flying Deuces,* despite the fact that I had been proved wrong in my first encounter with him, I still kept on disliking him, and I mean disliking him all the way. Basically, I couldn't understand why I felt as I did. He kept on being the most well-mannered, considerate, and gentlemanly person I had ever worked with, and it had become increasingly difficult for me to remember just what it was that had irked me so that first day.

I feel sure that it was Babe's eyes that finally won me over. I began to realize something I know to be true now— Babe had the softest, kindest, most expressive eyes I had ever seen in a human being. And those eyes, right up to the end, kept in them a certain naïve, little-boy look. I soon learned to read those eyes. Sometimes when I was out of sorts, I could see that twinkle starting to come, and I knew that I was in for a terrific teasing, and that I would have to wind up laughing with him.

But back to our first few meetings. As the picture went on, Babe realized that somehow he had offended me and he wanted to break down my haughty attitude toward him. As the picture went on shooting, I found it the most stimulating I had ever worked on. Stan and Babe were wonderful to work with. They were two of the hardest workers I had ever seen, but at the same time they seemed to get such great fun from their work. I think this is the sign of a really great comedian. They were helpful to the cast and crew always, but neither one could bear practical stupidity or carelessness.

They were both practical jokers, too. I found myself on the receiving end of a number of their pranks. By the finish of the picture, I knew that I liked them, and that working with them had been a great pleasure. As I got to know Babe better, I found many instances of his thoughtfulness and concern for others. One day on the *Saps at Sea* set, I slipped on a rolled-up carpet, fell backward, hitting the camera and suffering a slight concussion. Babe sent me an enormous box of red roses with a very nice but a very formal note wishing me a speedy recovery. (Years after, when we were married, Babe would ask me how and when I ever fell in love with him. I would tease him by saying it must have been when I fell and cracked my head.) When I received those flowers, I just thought it was another typically considerate thing that he did, nothing more. It wasn't until a few weeks later, in the second week of December, that I realized with stunning suddenness that this was something more than a very pleasant business association. We had never been out together and we had never seen each other except at work. Two days before Christmas, we became engaged. We had our first date on New Year's Eve and were married March 7, 1940.

Sincerely,
Lucille

16 December 1958

Dear Lucille:

I was very pleased to get details on Babe's working habits. It always struck m , as rather unusual that he didn't watch his own films too frequently. At least, I think I remember his telling me that. Is that true, and along the same line, what did he do for relaxation?

Sincerely,
Jack

4 January 1959

Dear Jack:

You're quite correct. He rarely watched the Laurel and Hardy pictures, especially in later years. He never liked watching himself on the screen. He did have his favorites among the pictures: *Babes in Toyland, Way Out West, Swiss Miss, Pardon Us, Bonnie Scotland,* and others of the short features that he would talk about from time to time. He particularly liked the L & H pictures which had "production." These are the ones that incorporated more than straight comedy. He always felt that in feature films the comedy should be incidental to the story and over-all production—that the comedian or comedians shouldn't be forced to carry the whole load of the film. When they did, he felt, the comedy element would become monotonous to the viewer. He dreaded previews of their pictures and rarely attended them. He relied on the reports from Stan, the studio executives, and myself. The fact that he concealed this dread from others led to the incorrect assumption by some people that he was disinterested—but this wasn't so. That fear was always with him although he had been able to overcome it to a certain extent in his earlier years. During his formative days, when he was perfecting his technique, he would watch his performances on film, both in the projection room and at *premières*. Until he finally established his complete style, he watched carefully in order to improve and further develop his mannerisms and characteristics.

And, as for relaxation, well, he loved to watch other comedians, for one thing. (On radio and television, his favorite programs were comedy and musical shows.) His favorite comedians were W. C. Fields, Fred Allen, Jimmy Durante, Ed Wynn, Jack Benny, Will Rogers, Charlie Chaplin, George Burns, Jackie Gleason-Art Carney, George Gobel, and Jack Paar. He could spot new talent instantly. He saw George Gobel on his first TV show and liked his fresh, clean style. I'm sorry Babe didn't live to see Jack Paar's success. It would have pleased him very much. He couldn't understand why Paar was just being given replacement work or why people apparently couldn't see his cleverness and potential. I'm sure Jerry Lewis would have been included in the list above if Babe had been able to see his development. He always liked Jerry but not the kind of things he was doing. He felt that talent was there but that Jerry hadn't found himself.

About Babe's hobbies. Outside of his natural curiosity and genuine interest in people (he loved people and life; in a way, *people* were his hobby), he had a great number of hobbies. I think, in fact, that his hobbies revealed more of him as a human being than his career did. *I feel that he felt and believed deep down that his hobbies and outside interests were the real Oliver Hardy*—and that his career was make-believe in every sense of the word.

He loved football, played it in school and with the Lubin company in Florida. Followed all college and professional games closely, attending whenever possible. USC was "his" team; for over twenty years he had a standing bet on USC in the annual big game against UCLA. He loved baseball, too. In Hollywood he played on the Vitagraph studio team, and all his life followed professional ball clubs, his favorite being the old Brooklyn Dodgers. He attended games whenever possible, listened to them on radio, watched them on TV. He was a great boxing fan. He loved sports of all kinds, really, and invariably pulled for the underdog when his own favorites weren't involved. But of all the sports in the world, none could compare with golf in his affections. This was a game he could play—and really play well.

He had belonged to a number of good clubs before he joined the Lakeside Golf Club in the San Fernando Valley around 1930, but it was at Lakeside that he did most of his playing, and he had a tremendous love and feeling for the club. He played golf with a vengeance when he got going. He would play 27 to 36 holes daily when not working at the studios. When he was working, if there were a few hours of daylight left, he would get in at least 9 holes before the dark stopped him. He frequently played foursomes with W. C. Fields, and it was here that he was confirmed in his opinion that Fields was one of the most naturally funny men he had ever seen. He golfed with Bing Crosby, Grantland Rice, Guy Kibbee, Babe Ruth, and others who were very good—so it's no wonder that in time he became very adept at the game. In the mid-thirties he won the Motion Picture Golf Tournament, defeating Adolphe Menjou in the finals.

He had so many enthusiasms, so many ways in which to live life to the fullest. He was a superb card player (he had learned as a boy when working at his mother's hotel). He had a natural opportunity to learn what with the traveling salesmen, theatrical people, and even occasional card sharps who turned up as guests. He did a lot of hunting in the early thirties—duck and quail mostly—and it wasn't until 1937 that his hunting activities were stopped—for good. He and Guy Kibbee went deer hunting in the Kaibab National Forest of Utah, and on the second day out he shot his deer. He ran over excitedly, looked at the dying animal, and it seemed as if the deer's eyes were reproaching him. He felt like a criminal, and never again lifted a gun.

He loved horses and the excitement of the track. He had a stable of his own, and like any venture which appealed to him, he went "all-out" in his excitement. He bought the works: horses, trainer, contract jockey, groom, exercise boy. But it was a terrible expense. To begin with, he knew nothing of the business end of it, and then, too, more often than not his horses were entered on the days when he was working. Most of his horses were clinkers (I recall that he did have *some* good ones), and he always bet on his own horses even if he knew they would be hopelessly outclassed. To him, this was a natural act of loyalty. As I said, it was an expensive hobby, and the whole thing ended one day when his favorite, Manny, was entered in a good claiming race. Babe was held up in a traffic jam on his way to Santa Anita and wasn't able to put a good bet on Manny. Manny won, and to top it all off, he was claimed by someone else. Babe gave up horse racing.

Babe was a farmer in a small way, too. He took up gardening partly because it was a necessity during the war.

We owned a three-acre farm in the San Fernando Valley and competent help was scarce. We became fired with patriotic enthusiasm to grow our own, so he proceeded to buy a shelf of books on Victory Gardening, animal husbandry, etc. He planted a half acre in vegetables—we already had a lot of citrus trees—and bought a flock of close to a hundred chickens. Then, because the settings didn't hatch soon enough, he got an electric brooder and stocked it with broods of day-old chicks. Next came turkeys and ducks. A friend gave us a cow, and Babe finally had to give it away, which he did reluctantly, only after the cow practically stripped all our fruit trees. In place of the cow, he bought a pair of piglets, and he tried to get a pair of lambs. I put my foot down about the lambs.

He really became involved in this new hobby, with the result that we wound up with a gigantic surplus of everything. There was an overabundance of fruit, vegetables, eggs, and chickens. We kept our friends supplied but even then we had too much. Then, of course, the inevitable happened. We made such friends of the chickens, ducks, and turkeys that we couldn't bear to kill them and eat them. We actually had to go out and *buy* fowl whenever we wanted it for the table. The pigs, too, became great pets. They followed us around like dogs and by the time they were full grown, they would practically knock us off our feet in their playfulness. We wound up giving the pigs away, too.

Farming led Babe into carpentry and here he became very expert. He built furniture, interior as well as exterior, in a very complete and well-equipped workshop. I can remember one anecdote about his carpentry that showed him at one of those rare times when he hadn't planned things very well. During our "farming" days, he decided to build some nests for our chickens, so he got my brother and a friend of his interested in the project. Neither of them knew any more about it than Babe. It was summer—and too hot to work in the sun—so they went to work in the theater we had on our property (called the Laurel and Hardy Fun Factory) which was built of tile and concrete, and comparatively cool. They hammered and sawed in there for two days, playing the radio, drinking cold beer to beat the heat—and then I was told one day, "Mission accomplished." I was summoned. They really did a good job of it, not quite professional looking, but really impressive. Then they started to move it out, and, just like in a Laurel and Hardy movie, it was too *big* to move out. They solved the difficulty, though. Babe removed a little porch he had built on each nest, and the henhouse moved out easily. Naturally, the porches had to be put back on again afterward. I don't think the hens appreciated the boys' handiwork nearly as much as the boys did.

And then there was Babe's *continuing* hobby, you might call it—cooking. As shown by his size and weight, he was quite a gourmet. He enjoyed good food and liked to prepare it. His top-notch specialties were spaghetti and meat balls (special grind and combination of meat, seasoned just so: the sauce took almost an entire day to prepare and cook); hamburgers (special grind again and his own special blend of seasonings); waffles (no ready-made mixtures for him: his were as light as air); and last of all, his Caesar salad. Scrumptious is the only word for it. He collected recipes and tried them out, always with a true chef's success.

So, you see, he was even a professional when it came to relaxing!

Sincerely,
Lucille

15 January 1959

Dear Lucille:

It's sometimes said that a professional comedian is rarely as funny offstage as he is on. Was this true of Babe? What was his personal sense of humor like when he was away from the lot?

Sincerely,
Jack

23 January 1959

Dear Jack:

Well, he certainly could be funny away from the studio, although, of course, he wasn't funny in the same way as he was before the cameras. He had a very quick wit and he was one of the few people I have known who could really take as well as give when it came to jokes. Being from the South and having the true Southerner's great affection for the South and its Negroes, he always enjoyed telling Southern dialect and Negro stories. (Babe had been practically raised by a colored mammy whom he called Mama. He called his mother Miss Emmy until he was old enough to know better.) Having worked for so long in minstrel shows, he knew how to tell Southern stories. I'll never forget one of his favorites which he could tell magnificently:

A gracious old Southern colonel had a wonderful slave

named Sam who had the best memory of anybody in the entire South. The two had been raised together and loved each other dearly. Sam idolized the colonel and the colonel thought the sun rose and set on Sam. After the war, Sam refused to leave the colonel and the colonel couldn't think of life without Sam so he decided to give him a piece of ground in order to keep him with him. Sam's reputation both for his devotion to the colonel and his prodigious memory gained fame throughout the South until one day even the devil heard about it. The devil tried every possible way to get Sam away from the colonel but could never succeed. Finally the colonel made a bargain with the devil: if the devil could prove that Sam's memory had failed—if he could prove that Sam had forgotten *anything*—then the devil could have Sam.

For years the devil tried everything he could to make Sam forget but nothing seemed to work. One day when the colonel and Sam were well along in years, Sam was hoeing in the garden and the devil popped up and said, "Sam, what'd the colonel have for breakfast this morning?" "Eggs," said Sam, and went on working.

Many years later when Sam and the colonel were very, very old men, Sam once more was working in the garden when up came the devil again. He said to Sam quickly, "How?" and without looking up, Sam answered, "Fried"—and the devil never pestered them again.

Babe also retained a number of old Southern sayings which he would quote when needed. I remember a few of these. If it rained while the sun was shining, he said, "The devil's beating his wife!" If his nose itched, he'd always say, "Someone's coming with a hole in his britches!" He particularly liked jokes and stories that incorporated a play on words. Loved puns, the worse the better, and loved the derisive reaction he got from others when he pulled them. He did this, of course, to people he knew didn't like puns. This stemmed from his love of teasing. He never allowed himself—and couldn't bear anyone else—to tell off-color jokes in mixed company. If anyone ever did in his presence, he never hesitated to call them down. Every woman, he felt, no matter what she was like, should be treated as a lady. She, in turn, should act as one at all times. He had the true Southern gentleman's great respect and reverence for womanhood. He always felt that a lot of that respect had gone out of the world.

Sincerely,
Lucille

3 February 1959

Dear Lucille:

I think I've obtained from you almost all the colorings of Babe's personality and character that are possible to be determined in this way. However, perhaps your patience with my questions won't be unduly strained if I ask you just one more. I would like to know Babe's essence, his spirit—his inward quality as a man. I know that's not easy to put down in words, but what would your description be of the man inside? For this, and for so much more, thanks, thanks, from

Yours ever,
Jack

17 February 1959

Dear Jack:

If I had to describe the real Babe to anyone, I'd have to point these things out about him. First of all, he was *naturally* gracious and courtly in manner. Even in those early years when he was playing heavies, he was always instinctively polite. One of his early directors suggested that he exaggerate this gallantry and see what the effect would be. He did, and much to Babe's surprise and the delight of others, it evoked laughter. This actually was the beginning of one of his strongest mannerisms in comedy. Because of his natural gentlemanly instincts, it was easy for him to follow this type of characterization, and to build and improve on it. He was by nature timid, sentimental, and *extremely* sensitive. To hide this, he sometimes affected a blustering, aggressive, almost gruff exterior to hide the inner inadequacy he sometimes felt. He was quick tempered but just as quick to get over it, and he never carried a grudge. He was very decided in his likes and dislikes, and sometimes he could be decidedly opinionated and stubborn.

This inner inadequacy I've mentioned was deep-seated. The occasional aggressive, bullying front he would put up to hide this was seen through by all the people who really knew him well. One of the biggest reasons for his inner feeling of inferiority and confusion was the simple fact that he hated being fat, and was very self-conscious about it. He was a big man, six feet two inches tall, and had weighed over 200 pounds all his adult life. He had weighed up to 350 pounds for a period in later years before illness struck him down. When people would comment on his size as often happened—particularly by fans and reporters when we were on tour—

they never knew or realized how much it embarrassed him or how upset he'd get. Most people were really astonished to see how tall he was, so that even when their remarks were about that, he still felt they were talking about his weight. He felt they were ridiculing him and so he, in turn, would ridicule himself. He was big and he didn't like it.

His size made him very conscious of his appearance, and that in turn made him very conscious of his dress. He was always meticulous in appearance. Due to his girth, he had to have all his clothes made to order but he didn't stop there. They had to be tailored to perfection and he always kept them spotlessly cleaned and pressed. He felt there was nothing worse than to see a fat man sloppy and careless in dress.

He felt his inadequacy in another way. He deeply regretted his lack of education and often said that he should have stayed longer in school. In order to overcome this, he read a great deal, all current events periodicals, biographies, stories of adventure, history, science. He seldom read fiction unless it was based on fact or historical incident. He also read books on law, real estate law particularly, on the growth and development of industry, etc., and, at least in later years, read the Bible a great deal.

I think a very important fact must be remembered about his relationship with Stan and the reason for his not entering more into the active end of creating the pictures. He had great admiration for and complete confidence in Stan's ability for "feeling" comedy situations and constructing them. This Babe felt even to the extent of belittling his own ability and ideas. Even when he felt inside himself that something wasn't just right, or that a situation as written just wouldn't play right, he would refuse to say anything to Stan or the writers about it. His contention was always, "Stan knows better than I do." He felt that if the thing was wrong, Stan would see it eventually and put it right. "Besides," Babe often said, "a person has no right to tear anything down unless he can offer something better to replace it." And true to Babe's predictions, in such instances, Stan would suddenly see on his own the faults Babe had talked about, and then he'd work out a solution to the problem.

Often this solution would come as they were doing a scene. They would each get the right feel of it, sometimes while the cameras were actually rolling. They would do whatever came naturally to the two characters they were portraying, and as they went through the scene, they would improvise, build, and develop just as it came to them. Some of their classic scenes happened in just that way. But even then, Babe never felt any credit was due him, or that he had any real part in the creating. He felt that he was merely following Stan's lead. Babe always felt that Stan was the brains and the comedian of the team, and that he himself was only the fall guy—the straight man for Stan—a small cog in the wheel. He never truly considered himself a comedian at all, and he was genuinely surprised that people thought of him as such. In his own mind, he felt his own characterization was merely supporting the comedy, not furnishing it. He felt that he was only a prop for Stan, and that he was, in his small way, making Stan and the situation funnier. This was typical of the *genuine* modesty of the man.

I received a letter the other day from Mrs. James Arata of Cincinnati, Ohio, a lady who worked with Babe years ago in his Florida days. She was Margaret O'Connor then, and worked as a singer in a club that all the film people went to in the evening. The description she gives of Babe in those days is one that you would use of him all through his life, right up to the end. Among a lot of other things, she said: "There never was anyone in the world as kind and softhearted as he. There was a very young married couple in Jacksonville who were singers. They had traveled through the South on a motorcycle, looking for work, and were terribly hard up. Babe took them in, got them a room at the hotel, and found work for them. They idolized him. Lucille, please, whoever portrays Babe if a picture is made—be sure that he is a down-to-earth human being with a soul and that certain look in his eyes. One thing keep uppermost in your mind. Anyone who plays Babe must have a beautiful tenor voice and a commanding personality. Above all, there must not be one tiny little thing phony about him—and where in the hell are you going to find him?"

And I suppose that's as good a way as any to end my reminiscences about him. You really can't sum up a man like that in just a few words, but if I had to, I'd repeat that statement one sometimes hears about a wonderful man who has passed on, and it fits because, above all things, Babe was gentle. The statement is: "He was a gentleman. He was a gentle man."

Yours sincerely,
Lucille

Chapter III

THALIA
AND
MR. ROACH

On one of his last journeys to the United States, Dylan Thomas was invited to participate in a recondite roundtable held by Cinema 16, a New York film society. An earlier portion of the evening had been devoted to the showing of the films of Maya Deren, a pioneer in what might best be called the esoteric film. Miss Deren in speaking of her films made the point that drama in a film is horizontal and that poetry in a film is vertical. Thomas listened to this and similar pronouncements, chain-smoking, and obviously unnerved by what he had been hearing. When his turn to comment came, he arose and said that he did not understand the particular reference to poetry in the film. "But," he said, "I know there *is* such a thing as poetry in the film. I can't give you a scholarly definition, but I can give you an instance. I remember once a scene in which Laurel pushed Hardy down the stairs—" Here he spluttered into laughter. "Ah, but I can't describe it. It would have to be seen. I say this only: that it was genuine poetry in every sense."

Some years later when Stan Laurel was told the story, he looked properly solemn. "Yes?" He looked more solemn and took a beat for the proper timing. "The hell he says!" Then, a loud volley of laughter and the matter was forgotten.

That the films of Laurel and Hardy appeal equally to one of our major poets and uncounted children (as the recent incredible upsurge in television showings attest) is a matter worthy of investigation. When the final countings are all in, moreover, it is a fact of note that the three comedy figures in the history of the cinema whose films have played more places more times to more people than anyone else's have

Arthur "A. J." Jefferson. Actor, playwright, producer, he was also an agile comedian, a master showman—and an exceptionally warm human being. His son Stan inherited these traits and with them the red hair and mobile face.

Stan Jefferson, 1906. In all senses of the word, a "boy" comedian. The gesture and the "Oops-what-have-I-done?" look was to stay with him well into the film days. The Chaplinesque umbrella cane was a standard English music hall comedian's prop.

Members of the cast of Fred Karno's *A Night in an English Music Hall* at sea prior to landfall in America. The handsome youth wearing the life preserver is Charlie Chaplin and the lad kneeling extreme left is his understudy, Stan Laurel.

Arthur Dandoe and Stan in *The Rum 'Uns from Rome* during a one-night stand at the Old Vic.

Stan and the Hurleys—"The Three English Comiques." Vaudeville days, 1914. Later known as The Keystone Trio.

Babe as a babe. His sister remembers him as ". . . a genuinely beautiful baby who loved everybody." Neither the years nor excess weight were ever to alter the essentially handsome cast of his features.

Babe is dominant in this picture of Lubin's football team, Jacksonville, Florida, 1914, and for good reason. Quick, light on his feet, he was the team's best player. The general appearance of fatigue suggests that Kalem Studio gave them quite a battle and some of the uniforms would indicate that part of the game was played underwater.

Ollie stares unbelievingly at Stan's "eyesie-earsie-nosie" routine in *Fra Diavolo*. Unbelief leads to emulation and angry frustration.

Ollie's camera look as he listens to Stan's detailed confession to their wives that they sneaked off to a convention (*Sons of the Desert*).

Babe as an opulently caparisoned lady of sorts, Lubin Pictures, 1915. The attitude of highly defensible virtue was a vital element of film comedy in those days.

Stan's first visit at Roach Studios to sign a contract, 1920. He appears to be exactly what he was—a natty vaudevillian hoping for better days.

Babe, Hal Roach, and Stan enjoying a between-scenes break on the set of *Our Relations*. Always on excellent terms, they were never close. They shared the usual employer-employee relationship with one vital difference: the boss let the boys do what they wanted before the camera. For this alone, film comedy is deeply indebted to Hal Roach.

These were *de rigueur* off-the-set togs in the early thirties. Stan and Babe were always well-tailored when not before the camera. What was perhaps usually not noticed about Babe in the films was that, despite his fat, he had a solid athletic build—the result of much golf and frequent dips into lakes of water, oil, molasses, and mud.

Glorious, splendidly eyebrowed Jimmy Finlayson and the beginning of his heroic "double-take and fade-away."

A minatory Hardy listens to the Laurel "cry" of apology. Stan is forgiven until the inevitable next time one reel later.

The notorious bandit, Fra Diavolo (Dennis King), reveals his plan to drug the wealthy Lord Rocburg as a prelude to robbery. Diavolo's faithful henchmen listen intently with looks of perfect comprehension. This means that not only will Lord Rocburg *not* be drugged but that Stan will inadvertently drink the potion himself thereby lousing up a magnificent bit of larceny. The boys, be it remembered, were dragooned into being bandits on the threat of death. The evil in their hearts, to vary the Shakespearean phrase, would not clog the foot of a flea.

If Ollie is going to commit suicide in order to forget his faithless girl, it is sound Laurel and Hardy logic that Stan go with him (*The Flying Deuces*). Shortly after this moment, Reginald Gardiner convinces Ollie that the Foreign Legion is the sovereign balm for hurt hearts. Happily, Ollie tells Stan to "throw that thing away!" Stan (having untied himself meanwhile) does, and Ollie gurgles down to the bottom of the river.

Stan is appalled at Finlayson's strenuous villainy in forcing Ollie into his cell (*The Flying Deuces*). A few moments later, a giant moment of comic lunacy is reached when Stan consoles his buddy (they have been sentenced to the firing squad at daybreak) by strumming "The World Is Waiting for the Sunrise," à la Harpo Marx, on the springs of an old army cot.

Ollie recumbent against the demon machine *(The Music Box).* No one in film comedy's history ever labored so mightily for his paycheck.

Another demon machine—high above an Alpine gorge *(Swiss Miss).* In less than a minute they meet the ape with truly devastating results.

Stan's astounding (and only) complete change of personality (*A Chump at Oxford*). After an amnesia spell, he is revealed to be Lord Paddington, Oxford's brightest scholar. The dean (Wilfred Lucas) has come to ask His Lordship if he can find time in his busy schedule to give Professor Einstein a few moments to help clear up an abstruse point in the relativity theory. Stan *thinks* he can find a moment or two; Ollie stands by with disapproving incredulity.

Three babes in the woods . . . with only one difference: the little girl (Jacquie Lyn) is a bit brighter than her chums (*Pack Up Your Troubles*). Like most studio stills this one has very little to do with the film. Actually, the child lulled Stan to sleep by finishing the bedtime story he had begun for her while Ollie was away.

"Serene at seventy" might serve as the caption here, if one were in a soulful mood.

In the same mood, one might call this ". . . and together forever" — and one might well be right.

been those of Charles Spencer Chaplin, Stan Laurel and Oliver Hardy.

Today, over twenty years after the making of their last film,* Laurel and Hardy are receiving almost as much fan mail as they did in their so-called days of glory. The television revivals in America account for much of the mail, but in almost every part of the world, in Ghana, in India, in Afghanistan, the image of the fat man and the skinny man haunt the consciousness of thousands of people. An English businessman told Stan Laurel some years ago that in an obscure village in China's heartland, placed prominently in the prayer room of a large house in the midst of the household deities on the altar, rests a picture of Laurel and Hardy. They are worshiped by the villagers as a symbol of China: the fat, all-knowing, well-fed mandarin side by side with the humble, ever-patient, underfed peasant who bears the burden of life with simple and happy placidity. Whether this custom has survived in the China of today is not known, but one of the modern public buildings in a large inland city still bears their picture painted three stories high where it stands for perhaps no other reason than that the natives like to look at it. France's gift of a television station to the Vatican included as its first film a Laurel and Hardy comedy. For relaxation between war travails both Stalin and Churchill were fond of screening their comedies, and today Marshal Tito has a very large library of their films which he sees over and over again. These wide-ranging instances of their popularity can be multiplied *in extenso*. It is enough to point out that wherever Laurel and Hardy are shown today, they are as popular as in their days of active film-making and in those places where they are still seen infrequently, their memory burns bright.

David Robinson, the noted film scholar, in a brilliant article on Laurel and Hardy in the British magazine, *Sight and Sound,* makes the point:

"Among the larger talents of the comedy film, Laurel and Hardy still remain outside the pale of the intelligentsia's recognition. They had their day of cultural respectability; and some have never deserted them. After *Laughing Gravy* (1931), *The Music Box* (1932), and *County Hospital* (1932), hats were respectfully raised. But Mickey Mouse and Silly Symphonies forced them into feature-length comedies

*I am not including *Atoll K* (known in England as *Robinson Crusoe Land* and in the U.S. as *Utopia* which was made in 1950, and is, chronologically, the last Laurel and Hardy film. A poor and badly executed film, it did not receive general release, much to the relief of its stars.

which at first their invention could not sustain. Many turned
their backs then, too soon to notice the success of their best
features—*Way Out West, Fra Diavolo, Swiss Miss*. We took
their huge output for granted, and at last forgot them, so
that their final unhappy attempts at film-making and their
disappearance from the screen passed almost unnoticed.

"This is ingratitude.

"Laurel and Hardy have made too many films. They have
made bad films, and they admit it themselves. They are
neither one of them geniuses. But they are very, very good
clowns—and they made a real, and characteristically unas-
suming, contribution to screen comedy."

Let us try to assess that contribution.

Great comedy must have an immediately identifiable quotient of style. Talent is essential but it needs line, definition,
form to make it truly memorable. ("Form," in these pages, is
used in an extended sense of that word to mean the thing or
things that are at once the comedian's style and content, his
exterior and interior characteristics—in short, his artistic
essence.) In mid-century United States, as perhaps in every
other country in the Western World, comedy is as much a
business of the film as it has ever been. Certainly a listing of
new releases in the trade journals show as high a proportion
of comedies as has ever existed in any given year. The one-
and two-reeler comedies are all but extinct, yet Mr. Magoo
and Bugs Bunny flourish mightily. Still, seemingly, the day of
the great film comedian, if not over, is at least in abeyance.
Chaplin is over seventy and sometimes seems determined to
settle the problems of the world by adding messages to his
comedies, which might be described as medicine-coating the
sugar. W. C. Fields, Harry Langdon, and Oliver Hardy are
dead; along with Stan Laurel and Harold Lloyd, Keaton is
largely inactive in films; the Marx Brothers have scattered. In
their places in recent years we have had Abbott and Costello,
Red Skelton, Bob Hope and Bing Crosby, Martin and Lewis
(together and single strength). Taking an open-minded attitude and saying that some of these comedians have potentially as much talent as their predecessors, we are aware immediately of one tremendous difference.

The difference is in *form*. The modern screen comedian
lacks it. Jerry Lewis, for example, is a performer with great
talent, although it may be too early to assess him fully. His
great lack is in form. Like Stephen Leacock's fabled knight,
he mounts his horse and rides off madly in all directions at
once. The keystone of a great comedian's talent lies in his

form: Chaplin's might be said to be his ludicrous dexterity in keeping alive Everyman's solitary, undaunted battle against the despoilers of a fresh and free earth; Keaton's, his infinite undertones and overtones of solemnity contrasted with his clown-acrobat attempts to make the impossible possible; Langdon's, his eternal inquisitiveness and innocent mischievousness—and the like.

This form is attained by sweat. Thalia is a hard task mistress and the most demanding of the Muses. Not one of the great film comedians of the past ever attained his majority suddenly. Nor, for that matter, does any artist. Is it because Hollywood has become so intrinsically an industry that there is no opportunity for the gradual development of an artist today? Is it because the old training grounds are gone, that we do not laugh as much when we see films today? Was the day vaudeville died the dawning of the death-day of the great comedian? These are probable answers the modern comedy film-maker would give in answer to the charge that people don't roar any more in the cinema. If this is a permanent condition, then it is a day of locusts and we are much the poorer for it.

The form that Laurel and Hardy took is not easy to outline. It might well be said that they had no form at all if one were asked for a succinct definition for the Encyclopaedia Britannica. The idiosyncrasies of the two men as they lope through their nether world of idiocy can be pinpointed but is there any unity to the whole? One feels there is, ranging widely and freely—although perhaps, like laughter itself, it may not be amenable to classification. But the attempt to distinguish that unity is an elemental part of the story these pages tell.

The only biographical material used herein is principally that which appertains to the creation of the comedy style of Laurel and Hardy. One recalls that some of the writers who have examined Chaplin's films have felt that every known detail of his private life placed in juxtaposition to his working life has significance. It may be so. The man and the artist are not inseparable but that they are solidly linked one to the other, ending in artistic effect, has always seemed to this writer debatable at best. In treating of certain periods of the personal lives of Stan Laurel and Oliver Hardy, this question has always been asked: In what way did this help them create the comedy that has given them a durability and an appeal second only to Chaplin's?

Let this serve, then, as a biography of the making of the

films of Laurel and Hardy. It is their story as comedians. It is also the story of some of their fellow workers who helped them attain the prominence that has diminished but very little through the years since the day in 1926 when the first Laurel and Hardy film was made on the Hal Roach lot at Culver City. And of all the men who worked with them none was more important to them or had less to do with their actual creative work as comedians than the man who first brought them together and signed their paychecks for over twenty years.

Hal Eugene Roach was born in Elmira, New York, January 14, 1892, exactly four days before Babe Hardy was born. This parallel between the two men is not the only one. Both were big men; both had a zesty, Falstaffian respect for life; both would rather have played golf than do almost anything else; both enjoyed a gag—and both lived life so fully and so enjoyably that they rarely spent much time in creating them. In this respect, they part definite company with Stan Laurel, who from the beginning of the films they all made together was almost a compulsive gag man, a plotter of plots without parallel, and one of the most untiring artists on behalf of a laugh that the film world has ever seen.

The late Charley Rogers, a director and gag man who worked closely with the three men for many years, says: "They were quite a bit alike, Babe and Hal. Stan was totally different from either of them. And yet there was a curious amalgam formed by the three of them that was pure gold coin. Roach had a terrific ability to spot talent. He knew what a good gag was but he usually let someone else work it out. He'd get an idea, talk it over with us, and then when it came to actually putting the gag on film, he'd say, 'That's the idea, boys. Work it out. Know what I mean?' Then he'd walk away and too many times we didn't know what he meant— not that that ever stopped us. As for Babe Hardy, he was good-natured, but by temperament somewhat easygoing. He was an artist to his fingertips once he got going, though. And when the shooting was over, back to the golf club. I don't know what would have happened to the Laurel and Hardy films if it hadn't been for Stan. He was the one who usually took an idea that Roach would have and bring it to life. He was usually the one who suggested to Babe the various things that could be done. In a sense, *he* is the spirit behind the films—but all of it could not have happened if those three men hadn't met at the right place and at the right time."

The right time was the Golden Era of the American comic

film. The right place was Hollywood, and in 1914 Hollywood was the right place for almost everybody to be. It was as yet, in most senses of the word, virgin territory. There was a newness and a healthy rawness, a basic and genuine sun-glitter far unlike the tinsel of later years. Hal Roach, after working in the Pacific Northwest and Alaska, drifted down the coast to the bright blaze of California and found it what he had always wanted. He got a job as a cowboy in J. Warren Kerrigan's Westerns which were then being filmed on the Universal ranch in the San Fernando Valley. Kerrigan took a liking to the young Roach and when the star went back to the studio in the city, he took the young ranch hand with him.

It was there, at Universal in 1913, that Roach met and became friendly with Harold Lloyd. They worked as extras most of the time, just getting by. For a while they worked as extras for a small company which was making L. Frank Baum's *Wizard of Oz* stories.

"One day," Lloyd says in his book *An American Comedy*, "Roach surprised me—though 'surprise' is a faint word for it, by announcing that he had got hold of several thousand dollars with which he intended making pictures of his own. A few days later, he rented a corner in the Bradbury mansion as an office, with the use of a stage in the backyard—and Hal Roach was a producer." Roach had an obsession that comedies featuring children would clean up on the market. He hired two boys and created a one-reeler around their foot loose shenanigans at the beach. Lloyd played the adult lead, a chauffeur who chaperoned the boys and was the butt of many of their deviltries. The film was not a great success but it was, of course, the seminal concept of the *Our Gang* comedies which were to enjoy such vast success in the twenties and early thirties.

Roach made a few more pictures with Lloyd but they parted amicably over details and Roach went on alone. Lloyd went over to Mack Sennett and Keystone and found that he was a small fish in a big pond. He had been much the whole show at Roach's although Roach was nowhere in sight of the title bestowed on him by Sennett in later years, "My only rival." Roach decided to reorganize his studio operations. He wanted a character—a comedian with form—a Chaplin figure, a Keystone Cop, anyone who would draw sequent numbers of audiences into the theaters. Lloyd returned. Their previous Lloyd character, Willie Work, had failed because he was not original nor particularly funny.

Roach and Lloyd came up with Lonesome Luke, a character they hoped would match Chaplin. The basic difficulty
with Lonesome Luke was that he *was* Chaplin—in reverse.
Every external identifying Chaplin characteristic was turned
about but it was the same old, eccentric, double-jointed
English music hall clown who emerged. Nevertheless,
Lonesome Luke became the staple of the Roach studio.
Pathé was the parent company; they bought Lonesome Lukes
as soon as they came out and were fairly well satisfied with
the product although no raging fires consumed the hinter-
lands as a result of their showing. The box-office grosses
were respectable but Lloyd gradually became aware in his
artistic conscience that Lonesome Luke was an essential
plagiarism and, consequently, foredoomed. He pleaded with
Pathé to allow him to make his own comedies in his own way.
"Simply," he said, "just myself—with maybe some slightly
different identification like horn-rimmed glasses."

The year was 1918. Roach had under contract a number
of other comedians he had been hoping to build up into
prominence. He had signed Toto, a prominent clown, to
make a series of twelve pictures, but after making seven,
Toto quit. The films were too confining to his free-wheeling
talents and he longed for the vast reaches of hippodromes
and tents. Alf Goulding, who had been alternating with
Roach in direction of the Lloyd films, had seen Stan Laurel
in vaudeville on the Pantages circuit. It occurred to him that
here might be the ideal comic to finish the remainder of the
Toto films and he suggested the idea to Roach. Roach, sight
unseen, wired Stan at the Santa Barbara theater where he
was appearing, asking him to report to the lot at seven
o'clock the next morning to appear as a comic waiter in a
film, as yet untitled and unplotted.

Stan's first fling in pictures with Ramish and Universal had
left an impression. "For one thing," he says, "and I'm quite
serious about it—it meant no more work at night. To get
away from barnstorming and hotel living was a big factor in
my decision to work for Roach. I went down to the studios
that next morning and played the part of a silly waiter in the
test film for Pathé. Pathé accepted it and I did five other
films, all one-reelers, and I can't remember a blessed thing
about them now. They had no particular plots. Just a funny
basic situation was necessary for those one-reelers and most
of the time you ad-libbed your comic bits as the camera was
turning."

Roach was impressed with the five one-reelers. He realized

that the soft-spoken young Englishman with the gracious manners was a born comedian. His mime was brilliant but what was equally important, he had a mind geared for comedy. He could improvise brilliantly and he lived and breathed in terms of funny situations. Stan completed his contract with Roach during this period when Lloyd was still the lot star. Then Stan went on to Vitagraph, working for Larry Semon, a former newspaper man and cartoonist, whose films were meeting with great success. Although not under contract, Stan did roles ranging from bits to full supporting leads in the Semon pictures at the rate of $10 a day. The procedure in showing "rushes" was to assemble three or four days' shooting at one time, run the rough sequence and show them to studio people. On one occasion, Antonio Moreno, the famous romantic star of the silent screen, happened by to see the rushes. He laughed immediately at Stan's antics and just tittered comfortably at Semon. At one point, he burst out with "This guy's funnier than Semon" which, of course, did not amuse Mr. Semon.

The following day, an important chase sequence in a Semon film, *Scars and Stripes,* was to be filmed. This had been planned as a fairly elaborate routine featuring both Semon and Stan as escaped convicts going through a series of comic misadventures. At the outset of the shooting, Semon insisted on his prerogative as star and rewrote the action. He had Stan tied to a tree with handcuffs, quite unable to escape, while Semon went on the chase by himself. Stan never worked again with Semon.

Back to vaudeville once more. Again the wheel had turned and the fortunes of Stan Laurel had made a circuit right back to the starting point. But before he once again wearily slapped more PANTAGES CIRCUIT labels on his trunks, Stan had an opportunity to make a quickie two-reeler for "Broncho Billy" Anderson, the one-time cowboy star, now a producer. The story was not much. The comic, played by Stan, finds a stray dog and enters it in a dog show, winning first cash prize. The owners show up, the comic is accused of theft but all ends happily. The picture, *Lucky Dog,* directed by Jesse Robbins, was made as a sample and sent East for possible release. To Stan Laurel at the time it was just another job but the film (which has since vanished) was important to cinema history; one of the actors supporting Stan was Oliver Norvell Hardy, fresh from a stint of labor with the redoubtable Semon. "Babe and I were friendly," Stan remembers, "but there was nothing about the picture or our own personal relationship to suggest that we might ever become partners. He and I were just two working comics, glad to have a job—any job." The actors were told that the picture was to be sent to the office of Metro Pictures in New York for screening and sales. As nearly as Stan could see it, this was to be his swan song in pictures.

Hal Roach, meanwhile, had started the full swing of his production career. The Lloyd films had brought him much attention and he began a dedicated attempt to gain equal footing with Mack Sennett, the unchallenged King of Comedy. An examination of the Roach films of this period show that he had a good, active concept of film comedy but showed uncertainties of execution. He needed more idea men and, above all, he needed an executive producer with vision and imagination to supervise the making of the films. Roach himself had a flair for comedy but what was wanted was a working producer to handle studio activities while Roach concentrated on selling the product. The man needed was the man found: F. Richard "Dick" Jones.

To old-timers on the Roach lot and to many people who were a part of the world of film comedy then, the name of Dick Jones was the symbol of absolute integrity in film comedy. A slender, intense man of medium height, he seemed to consume himself in creativity. Humor was the blessing of his existence and he strove mightily on its behalf. A stickler for thoroughness in his work, he had been production chief at Sennett's and, among other films, had directed Mabel Normand's delightful feature, *Mickey*. Then, and during his time with Roach as production head, he was unrelenting in pursuit of perfection. Stan remembers him with great affection: "I've never seen anyone work like him. I remember that when I joined his staff of writers and gag men, he took a liking to me and taught me a good deal. There was no such thing as regular working hours for him. It was a day and night job, Sundays included. He was the one who started me as a director. He gave me wonderful training and taught me a lot of tricks about the use of the camera. I've always felt grateful to him for his encouragement. He was a man with a brilliant mind and with greatly advanced ideas. I think you could say that he was really a genius. He certainly did a lot for the Roach studio. He drove himself continually until he became a nervous wreck. I'm sure that overwork killed him."

At the time Stan was on the long, long turn of the Pantages wheel, Babe Hardy was gaining recognition as an excellent heavy with various studios. He worked for Vitagraph and also as a heavy for Jimmy Aubrey, then making a series of two-reelers for Fox. He had appeared in a series based on the O. Henry stories for Earl Montgomery, an independent producer. But perhaps his best pre-Roach work was done with Larry Semon who had not found himself in harmony with Stan Laurel. The comedies of Larry Semon are rarely revived today even in this era of art film festivals and old-time comedy festivals, but in their own strenuous way they were excellent. Semon was basically a personality comedian, not much given to originality in comic concepts, but with an essential cleverness in the use of mechanical gags. His films found a consistent market. He was an affable man and an extravagant one. While under contract to Vitagraph, his pictures started off as money-makers but in time the profits diminished. Babe Hardy has explained why: "He helped bring about his own downfall. I can remember one instance that was typical. Understand this now. We were doing a two-reeler called *The Sawmill*. Just a regular two-reeler, to be done on a regular two-reeler budget, which wasn't a lot. But Larry took us up on location and I mean location. It was a North Woods picture, and Larry took a very big company up into the wilds of the California mountains. He built—believe it or not—he *built* permanent log cabins and buildings for a full company with all the comforts of life, and we spent about three months on that picture. Vitagraph after a while insisted that he become his own producer because they just weren't going to foot all those bills. And then when the bills started to come in, he'd worry—but then he was always worrying, and the funny thing is that he was never able to figure out why things weren't going well for him. We always had a lot of fun, and I loved working for Larry, but you can't have a lot of fun and make a lot of money—not under those conditions anyway."

Semon made a few memorable films on his own, *The Girl in the Limousine* and *The Wizard of Oz* among them (in which Babe was featured), and then he found to his horror that the releasing company, Vitagraph, was not accepting his films. His worrying deepened into a profound depression. Semon contracted tuberculosis and died in 1928.

Babe then went on to Fox and worked for W. W. "Woody" Van Dyke, who was directing Buck Jones cowboy films. After working as a heavy for Van Dyke, he was called to work by Roach on a two-reeler with Theda Bara, a star on the downgrade. "I had become the typical heavy," Babe has said. "I had a very beautiful sneer even if I say so myself. Outside of the work I had done in Florida and New York, I was in the habit of thinking of myself as a villain. About this time while I was working for Roach, the boys at the studio got a hint as to my possibilities as a comic. Dick Jones was directing *Rex, King of Wild Horses,* and I was made up as a typical heavy. I wore a patch, a scar, the whole picture of a villain. The camera was set up on a low level to emphasize my height at one point when I was supposed to ride up a sand dune and survey the scene below. I rode up the incline and stared ahead with a menacing look and just then—*whoomph*—my weight made the horse sink very slowly into the sand. The boys behind the camera couldn't go on because they were howling so much. We didn't do much work *that* day!" Roach was pleased with the prospect of having a man who could be very convincing as both a heavy and a comic. Babe signed a Roach contract.

Stan, after a year on the vaudeville circuit, returned to California in 1919 and was told by Broncho Billy that *Lucky Dog* after much examination and previewing had been accepted by Metro for release, and that similar ones were wanted. Anderson went into full production and signed Stan to a contract for a series of comedies. A number of these were designed to be parodies of famous full-length films of the time; Rudolph Valentino's notable *Blood and Sand,* for example, was done as *Mud and Sand,* featuring Stan as the immortal lover, Rhubarb Vaselino. This film proved so successful that a Robin Hood parody called *Rob 'Em Good* was announced in the trade papers as imminent in production. Whether by accident or design, the title, *Rob 'Em Good,* was also taken by the producers of Bull Montana's films at Metro Pictures for one of his two-reelers. The Metro film was also a Robin Hood take-off but Anderson decided to go ahead with his film anyway, retitling it, *When Knights Were Cold.*

"I wish they'd re-release *When Knights Were Cold,*" Stan has said. "I guess maybe I'd like to see it again because it has one beautifully funny sequence that I've never seen in movies—either before or since. We had an army of knights in a chase sequence. There were over three hundred of them working with basket horses—you know, the circus clown-type horses, with the men's legs extending beneath the little papier-mâché horse built around them. It was hilarious, like some of those circus routines. There were a lot of routines we did in those days that have been forgotten today. Comics now lean too much on the line gag and not the visual gag. I think

that Hollywood comics these days are talking too much and
not *doing* enough."

Anderson made a few more films with Stan before he
reneged on a contract detail regarding payment and Stan left
for his old standby, vaudeville. Hal Roach meanwhile had
seen the great success of *Mud and Sand,* and in 1920 sent for
Stan and asked that he sign for twelve one-reelers and twelve
two-reelers, some to be parodies; others, originals. Roach
also signed Will Rogers to do parodies (among them a
brilliant one spoofing Douglas Fairbanks's Robin Hood), and
Irvin S. Cobb, who was put to work at the studio in comedies
featuring his own name as the series title. The names of some
one- and two-reelers Stan did at this time for Roach suggest their spirit: *Under Two Jags (Flags), Rupert of Cole
Slaw (Hentzau), The Soilers (Spoilers), Wild Bill Hiccup
(Hickok).* Thalia never had it so good.

"The years around the early twenties are almost a kind of
blur to me now," Stan confesses. "I can remember it all in a
chronological order, of course, but I don't think I can really
recall anything unusual that would help explain the building
of the character I was to use when I was teamed with Babe.
I can recall a few interesting things, though, that did happen
before I joined Roach for good in 1926. For one thing, I
became a star!

"After my initial contract with Roach was finished, I fell in
with Joe Rock, a comedian in his own right, who got the idea
of making and producing comedies for himself. He wasn't
going to star in them, though. He had ideas for various series
but the one I was most interested in was a number of
two-reelers that he called the Stan Laurel Comedies. Gosh,
those were fun to make! Joe went to Universal for studio
space and in his rental fee he stipulated that he could use any
of the old Universal sets still in shape. Some of those sets
were massive—like the huge set for *The Hunchback of Notre
Dame,* the picture that starred Lon Chaney at his height. We
took that gorgeous set and used it for a two-reel take-off on
Dr. Jekyll and Mr. Hyde. We called it *Dr. Pyckle and Mr.
Pryde.* Pretty funny movie, too. We did that with other
elaborate sets, as well. I recall one particularly gorgeous one
that we used for *Monsieur Don't Care* which, of course, was
a parody on another Rudolph Valentino film, *Monsieur
Beaucaire.* The Stan Laurel Comedies went over well in the
trade, and Hal Roach approached me about coming back to
work for him."

The Hal Roach studio, at this time (1926), was a one- and

two-reeler factory. They were, as Stan recalls, rather good in the main. Some of course were potboilers but under the sure and controlling hand of Dick Jones, even the trite films had well-edited pace if nothing else. Roach at this time was wooing Thalia wisely but not too well. For all his own talent in finding talent, he had not developed a full-fledged comedy star with the box-office name of a Chaplin, Langdon, or Keaton. His one great accomplishment was the organization of what in effect would be known today as a stock company. He had under contract a number of versatile and talented comedians, none of them stars, but all devoted to comedy and able to execute it with sureness and dispatch. It was at this time that one of these comedians, the ineffable Jimmy Finlayson, made a name for himself under the Roach banner.

James Finlayson, who was to be in a sense to Laurel and Hardy what Margaret Dumont was to the Marx Brothers, was a Scotsman, born in 1881, 1884 or 1887 at Falkirk. The varying birth dates which Fin always gave suggest the faint air of mystery that always surrounded him. Fin did not like his age known period. Almost exactly the same person off-screen as on, he reveled in the job of making comedy. He went on the stage immediately after graduating from Falkirk College and appeared for a while in England before he came to America around 1910. After several years on the American stage, he made his screen debut in Jack Blystone's L-KO Comedies. Subsequently, he worked for Mack Sennett before starting work on the Roach lot in the twenties. From time to time he worked as a free-lance comedian for First National, Paramount, and RKO.

Roach in the mid-twenties was earnestly casting about for comedians of Chaplin stature. Lloyd and Toto had left for greener pastures. For a time in the early twenties, Roach tried to build Harold Lloyd's brother, Gaylord, into a comedy star but once again the public wouldn't turn out in sufficient numbers. Ever on the lookout for the genuinely novel, Roach attempted to make comedies with animals and in 1924 did a few films with monkeys acting as humans. A typical film of this period, *The Man Pays* (1924), is describable only as "cute." Roach called this animal troupe "The Dippy Doo-Dads" and in *The Man Pays* they enact all the silly and touching things that occur at a wedding. It is an interesting film but perhaps so only in the same fashion as Dr. Samuel Johnson's famous walking dog. At this time, too,

Roach teamed Earl Mohan and Billy Engle, two effervescent ex-vaudevillians, with adequate but not exciting results.

Undaunted, he began a series of comedies in 1926 with Jimmy Finlayson as star. Here possibly might be the new Chaplin, the big name to push Roach Studios above and beyond Keystone. Stan Laurel was hired at this time purely as a writer and a gag man. He was assigned by Dick Jones to write a scenario for a Finlayson one-reeler which would serve as a sample film—or in current television terminology as a pilot—for inspection by the releasing company, Pathé. This was Stan's first job as writer and director and he did well. The Finlayson was accepted by the releasers. Dick Jones liked the picture very much and asked Stan to work on the Clyde Cook film, then in work, which had received the separate attentions of fourteen directors. Clyde Cook, an Australian, after some success on the stage in the *Ziegfeld Follies* had been spotted by Roach as a possible star. A sharp-nosed, wiry little dancer and acrobatic comedian, Cook was known as "The Kangaroo Boy." He was an extremely talented comic but his first picture had not been accepted by the releasers, and Roach rightly realized that it was director trouble which had impeded its progress. Cook, although a good "natural" comedian, needed an expert hand to guide him. In the process of being remade by various directors, the scenario had become an almost hopeless jumble. Louise Fazenda had been added to the cast as "name" insurance but even this had not helped. Dick Jones now turned to Stan and asked him if he could bring order out of the chaos. After looking at the film, Stan realized that disorder was integrated into the entire film which by now had been stretched in footage to seven or eight reels. "Why not," asked Stan, "cut it up into five or six one-reelers?" Jones rejected this on the grounds that enough money had been spent already. Stan then suggested that the footage, much of which was funny but disconnected, be kept intact, but furnished with a prologue and an epilogue. The prologue consisted of a film writer calling on a producer (played by Max Davidson) who listens to the proposed scenario the author has dreamed up. The Clyde Cook footage was then run off and at its conclusion an epilogue brings us back to the producer's office. The producer, with glazed eyes, looks at the writer, pulls a gun from his desk and shoots him. Thus, with just a bit of comic thinking, a great deal of chaotic footage was made to seem purposeful and was saved for release. It is possible that W. C. Fields saw this film and relished the device because it is the same formula he used to reveal the plot of his own screen play, *Never Give a Sucker an Even Break*, featuring himself as the writer and Franklin Pangborn as the producer.

The project to make Finlayson a star languished, then died. Fin had style as a comedian but not enough. His form was rudimentary. Roach, in desperation, hit on the device of hiring "name" stars whose days of greatness were almost over, hoping that whatever was left of their glory might attract some people to the box office. During the middle twenties, Roach built comedies around Theda Bara, Agnes Ayres, Priscilla Dean, Harry Meyers, Herbert Rawlinson, and—as incredible as it may seem—Lionel Barrymore. It was in one of these "fading-star" pictures that Stan made a return to acting, never again to leave it. Oddly enough, he had to be forced to do the film.

For sometime he had been settling down comfortably at Roach's. Serving as a gag man, he had also directed a few of the "fading-star" films. One of these featured Harry Meyers (who later played the unforgettable drunken millionaire in Chaplin's *City Lights*). Babe Hardy had been cast as a timid butler. Cast call was for a Monday but on Sunday, Babe, whose hobby was cooking, scalded himself severely while laboring over a leg of lamb. In a frantic attempt to get a substitute, Dick Jones tried to get either Charlie Murray or Chester Conklin to play the part. They were unavailable. Frantically, Jones asked Stan to play the role but Stan refused. He had been assigned to direct the picture and he found writing and directing much more congenial than acting. Roach added his entreaties to Jones's and topped it with a $100 raise. Stan acceded, but with misgivings.

The picture, *Get 'Em Young*, was not a notable one and Stan does not remember much of the plot. "The only thing worth remembering about it, I guess," he says, "is that the part of the whimpering butler I played in it gave me the first real mannerism that definitely became a part of my later character when I was teamed with Hardy. In the film, I was a very timid chap, running around and reacting with horror to everything that went on around me. To emphasize this, I cried at one point, screwed my face up—and have used it ever since. Funny thing about that cry, though: it's the only mannerism I ever used in the films that I didn't like. I remember years later when we would be improvising something on the set and we came to a pause where we couldn't think of anything to do—or had a dull moment—Roach always insisted that I use the cry. It always got a laugh, and it sure became a part of my standard equipment, but somehow I never had any affection for it."

Following *Get 'Em Young,* Stan returned to his gag-writing duties, as he thought, for good. The next picture on the docket was to feature Priscilla Dean, Herbert Rawlinson, and Albert Conti. Stan was slated to write much of the film and had been at work on it when Jones asked him to write himself into it. Stan demurred strongly; again Roach rallied around with a $100 raise; again Stan stepped reluctantly before the cameras—this time to remain. The picture, *Slipping Wives,* was a story of an artist, his beautiful wife, and a cardboard lover in the person of a paint salesman who is used by the wife to arouse her husband's dormant passions. There was also a comic butler in the cast. The cardboard lover and the butler were the supporting players. The picture was of ordinary quality but the two supporting actors were not. One was Stan Laurel and the other was Oliver Hardy, and for the first time they were appearing together in a picture by Hal Roach.

Chapter IV

MR. LAUREL
AND
MR. HARDY

"Of all the questions asked about us," Stan Laurel says, "the most frequent is, how did the two of you get together? I always explain that we just sort of came together—naturally."

To amplify this, it should be said that the curious mixture that is Laurel and Hardy was not a contrived compound. Hal Roach did not sit down, strike his forehead and shout: "Stan Laurel and Babe Hardy—together! Why didn't I think of that before!" But perhaps he did something like that when he came to understand that on his lot he had two men who fitted together without a seam showing.

Laurel and Hardy were joined by accident and grew by indirection.

Roach's All Star Series was running out of stars. He had extracted box-office returns from former greats like Theda Bara and Lionel Barrymore, but it was a vein of value soon worked out. His active need was for a new star and he had not succeeded in creating one or a shadow of one. But he realized that he had a studio full of genuine artists, each in his own way a potential star. This realization brought about the creation of the Roach Comedy All Stars, and Laurel and Hardy were vital parts of the organization. They could and had played almost any part available in the Roach comedies. Neither one thought of himself as being a special kind of comedian. Each had learned his trade the hard way—the best way—by *doing,* by appearing in a variety of productions, live and filmed, under almost every conceivable kind of circumstance. Where one might be a hawk-beaked heavy one week, he might well have to be an amiable, pudding-faced red-nosed tramp the next. There was no type casting in those early days of comedy. "I don't know how to answer young comedians who ask me how they can learn their trade," says Stan today. "For one thing, I guess they just don't have the advantages today that we had. A friend once asked me what comedy was. That floored me. What *is* comedy? I don't know. Does anybody? Can you define it? All I know is that I learned how to get laughs, and that's all I know about it. You have to learn what people will laugh at, then proceed accordingly. First of all, you should start out, I think, with a fairly believable plot, no matter how broad it is, and then work on from there. But you've got to *learn* how to go on from there. Nobody's going to teach you. That's why one of the best ways for a young comedian to learn his trade is to get as much summer stock as possible, appearing in repertory, changing parts, being in different situations, over and over again until he learns the 'feel' of different audiences. He has to learn why certain gags go over, and why they *don't*. You develop an intuition after facing various types of audiences. What one will laugh at, another won't, and vice versa. One day you'll know. Then, you're in business."

In 1926, Laurel and Hardy were just a part of the Roach Comedy All Stars. They were integral to the group but did not consider themselves *the* stars. This recalls the story that swept through the rather special world of Gilbert and Sullivan actor-singers about a certain great G. and S. star who had insisted on getting more and more prominence in the famous company for which he worked. He was buttressed in his own very good opinion of himself by the undeniable fact that he was a fine singer and comedian. But the management did not give him the recognition he deemed proper. "No, Mr. X," said the producer. "You really must realize that there is room only for two stars in the company. One's name is Gilbert, the other's is Sullivan."

In 1926, Laurel and Hardy, like Gilbert and Sullivan, ham and eggs, and Rodgers and Hart came together—and neither of them had anticipated or particularly desired the conjunction. It was, in a sense, inevitable. Stan and Babe had talents superior to their fellow players. Neither of them actively promoted self-advancement but Hal Roach with his talent for organization and his ability to recognize gold when he saw it brought them together. It was a comparatively slow process initially; it was also simple mathematics. Quite unwittingly, almost unwillingly, their parts in the films became larger; the parts of the other players diminished. *Ergo sumus.* In 1926, Leo McCarey, who was to attain great fame in films by

making *Going My Way* with Bing Crosby, was a production
supervisor and some-time director for Roach. To him was
given the job of directing the first official Laurel and Hardy
film, *Putting Pants on Philip*. The film does not much resemble the Laurel and Hardy films of maturity. They were the
leads in this story because they fitted well together. Their
form was yet to be found.

Stan played a Scottish immigrant, attired in kilts and
tartan, who arrives at New York harbor. He is met by
Hardy, his American uncle, nattily attired in conventional
summer suit and sailor straw hat. Horrified at seeing his
relative attired in costume so obviously un-American, Uncle
takes Philip to a tailor for a new suit. Comedy in 1926 was
not always subtle, and in the scene in which the tailor
attempts to measure Philip's inseam length, the playing is
broadly hilarious. It was not, however, vulgar—if that can be
believed. What saved it from vulgarity is difficult to isolate
except that Laurel and Hardy have never been vulgar at any
point in their career. Search as one might through the films,
the purely suggestive is always absent. One cannot make films
for both children and adults and do otherwise, but clean
comedy was natural to both men. They despised smut. In
Putting Pants on Philip, when slapping down the tailor's hand
as he pulls up the skirt, Stan conveyed such a feeling of
innocent comic panic that the action is hilarious, not offen-
sive.

There is not much else to note of value in the team's first
film. During this time, the Roach Comedy All Stars were
producing a number of comedies which utilized the two boys
in leading roles, but which were not Laurel and Hardy
comedies. In 1926, the Comedy All Stars turned out most of
the total Roach product and Laurel and Hardy films were
looked on as potentially good but still rather much in the
nature of an experiment. *Putting Pants on Philip* was not
released for some months after completion because subse-
quent Laurel and Hardy films in work seemed to be likelier
vehicles for the box office. *Philip* was released only after a
number of their films had begun to attract movie-goers.
Laurel and Hardy were picked up by exhibitors slowly but
increasingly.

The Comedy All Stars continued during this period as
something very much like a permanent stock company, and
there seemed to be little formal plan for its *modus operandi*.
If Roach, Leo McCarey, Stan, or any of the gag men came
up with a good idea, it was talked over in conference and if

it seemed of general comic quality, it was developed for the All Stars. Laurel and Hardy were yet tentative in appeal.

A typical Comedy All Stars film made some time after the first Laurel and Hardy film, and important in a consideration of their history, was *Why Girls Love Sailors,* based on an idea of Roach's. Roach frequently came up with an excellent idea which he would give to the gag men and director with instructions to "work it out." This usually was a perfectly equitable and satisfactory arrangement but Roach also had the unpredictable habit of interfering during shooting and changing things unexpectedly. This comparatively harmless habit was not hurtful in the early days when the films were done quickly and without the fuller realism of the later pictures, but it did blunt the effect in some later Laurel and Hardy feature productions. Perhaps in those days, the word to be used was not "interfering" but "collaborating." It was a pleasant way of making a living. There was no regular schedule in the fullest sense of the word. An idea would be taken up and discussed without the fear that it had to be finished by a certain date. All hands joined in to create a full and powerful comedy, and good ideas were welcome. Roach's idea on this occasion was to do a burlesque of the heavy sailing melodramas then (1927) a favorite subject of the feature films. Babe Hardy was cast as a rough sea captain who kidnaps a lovely young lady and spirits her away to his ship. The girl's lover was Stan Laurel, playing a comparatively straight juvenile with comic undertones. Unable to best the captain in personal combat because of their obvious differences in heft, Stan utilizes strategy and masquerades as a Theda Bara-type vamp. The captain is much attracted to the new charmer and seems to be making great headway when his bargelike wife heaves in sight to confront him. She concludes the captain's discomfiture with her fists, and Stan escapes with the girl.

Why Girls Love Sailors is significant because it gave Babe Hardy one of his most durable and humorous trade-marks, the "tie-twiddle." In one sequence, he is walking along deck when he hears a tremendous racket going on inside a stateroom. He opens the door to quell the disturbance but is met with a pail of water in the face. "I was expecting it," Babe admitted later, "and yet in a way, I wasn't. I had a vague memory of it being part of the action coming up but as I recall I didn't expect it at that particular moment. It threw me mentally, just for a second or so, and I just couldn't think of what to do next. The camera was grinding

away, and I knew I had to do *something,* so I thought of
blowing my nose with my wet and sopping tie. I was raising
my tie to my nose when all of a sudden I realized that this
would be a bit vulgar. There were some ladies watching us.
So I waved the tie in a kind of tiddly-widdly fashion, in a
kind of comic way, to show that I was embarrassed. I
improved on that little bit of business later on, and I used it
for any number of situations. But usually I did it when I had
to show extreme embarrassment while trying to look friendly
at the same time. And that's how the tie-twiddle was born."
The variations on this simple movement are, of course, legion
throughout the long history of the comedies, and it was used
many times in an impromptu fashion. When Babe was confronted with some appalling situation (of which he was
usually guiltless), the tie-twiddle became his standard form of
expressing his reaction.

Another one of the Hardy stand-bys was born in the same
picture. "It seems strange that so many good things for me
could come out of the same film," Babe has said, "but it's a
fact that on that very set, in that very scene, just after I did
the tie-twiddle, I had to become very exasperated. So I just
stared right into the camera and registered disgust. The
camera kept on going, and in that way my slow burn was
born." The Hardy slow burn or "camera look" was to become as well known as the tie-twiddle and it, too, was subject
to infinite variations. Additionally, it helped to maintain a
more effective pace in the films by giving the audience time
to assimilate a comic detail and savor it.

In the 1927-28 period at Roach, a number of comedies
were made that contained the germinal situations for the fully
accomplished Laurel and Hardy films of later years. Repeating a plot was not and is not an unusual cinematic
custom, but repeating and improving a dozen-fold in every
area *is* unusual. Looking at the Comedy All Star's productions of *Love 'Em and Weep, Hats Off,* and *Duck Soup,* one
discovers the basic situations used in some fine Laurel and
Hardy films of the thirties, *Chickens Come Home, The Music
Box,* and *Another Fine Mess.* The difference between the
three pairs of films is essential: the early ones still show
much of the frenetic Sennett influence in which rapidity of
action was too often done for its own sake; the latter reveal
the leavening influence of two distinctive comedy characters
who impart the breathing touch of humanity to wild and
whirling deeds. It was the growth of this delightful sub-
human inhumanity that Stan Laurel was to learn how to

direct with increasing artistic vigor as he gradually grew to have more and more control over the films.

And Roach's Chaplin? He could never exist but Roach had found a curious mixture that added up to something which was attracting people in the way Chaplin was. Late in 1927, keeping *Putting Pants on Philip* in reserve, he announced to the motion picture industry the release of the Laurel and Hardy Comedies, and for first showings offered the exhibitors two films, *Let George Do It* and *The Battle of the Century*. *The Battle of the Century* was the second Laurel and Hardy film ever made, and oddly enough, it may have been the greatest.

The release of the new films found theater managers willing to buy. An editorial of a trade magazine of 1927, *The Exhibitor*, exhorted managers:

> The exhibitor can build up his attendance by featuring personalities and forgetting the "two reel" plug on the marquee ... The Stan Laurel and Oliver Hardy comedies were to be competitors of features. Then why not advertise these two personalities? Their latest, *Let George Do It*, caused trade paper representatives to holler right out in laughter, and when a comedy can do this then it must be good. So, Mr. Exhibitor, feature Stan Laurel and Oliver Hardy on your marquees. That is what is being done over the West Coast Theatre circuit by Harold B. Franklin, and he is cashing in.

Most exhibitors followed the advice; the Laurel and Hardy grosses began to mount, and Roach quickly sent *Putting Pants on Philip* on its way to the public. Of the three Laurel and Hardy films then in general release, it was perhaps the weakest in distinctive humor, and it was very much inferior to the second film they made.

Henry Miller, the part-time *enfant terrible* of American letters, is noted for writings other than *Tropic of Cancer* and *Tropic of Capricorn* which American tourists have been smuggling into the country for many years. He is also an essayist of note, and one of his most penetrating collections of notes is "The Cosmological Eye," published in London in 1945. In an essay on films, *The Golden Age*, he speaks of *The Battle of the Century*:

And after thousands of slap-stick, pie-throwing Mack

Sennett films, after Charlie Chaplin had exhausted his bag of tricks, after Fatty Arbuckle, Harold Lloyd, Harry Langdon, Buster Keaton, each with his own special brand of monkey shines, came the chef d'oeuvre of all the slap-stick, pie-throwing festivals, a film the very title of which I forget, but it was among the very first films starring Laurel and Hardy.

This, in my opinion, is the greatest comic film ever made—because it brought the pie-throwing to apotheosis. There was nothing but pie-throwing in it, nothing but pies, thousands and thousands of pies and everybody throwing them right and left. It was the ultimate in burlesque, and it is already forgotten.

But not quite.

One day at the studio while the gag men were sitting about discussing plot lines, someone came up with an idea for a film for Laurel and Hardy. The plot was a thin one but the idea man suggested an embellishment. "We could even slip a few pies into it and—" He was hooted down. Pies, after all, were pies. That was early Sennett, mid-Chaplin, and late everybody. This was 1927, an enlightened age. Despite this general reaction, Stan pondered the idea and brought forth what he hoped would be a variation good enough for consideration. "Look," he said, "if we make a pie picture—let's make a pie picture to end all pie pictures. Let's give them so many pies that there will never be room for any more pie pictures in the whole history of the movies."

His idea was accepted on general principle and gag men went to work. At the same time the purchasing agent bought the pies. Miller's recollection was not exaggerated. There *were* thousands and thousands of pies, and they were real pies, not studio substitutes. They were custard, cherry, blueberry, raspberry, coconut, banana, and lemon cream—the works. A total day's output of The Los Angeles Pie Company was purchased—four thousand pies. The *pies* were ready, but even a pie picture to end pie pictures needs a plot. Stan puts it in his own words:

"For some good reason that I can't think of at the moment, we decided that this should be a fight picture, and for that reason, and because of the gigantic pie conflict in it, we called it *The Battle of the Century*. Hardy is my manager; I

am a prize fighter. A packed arena. I came out for the first
round and get knocked out cold with one blow. Fade out.
Fade in. The arena again, only now it is completely empty. I
am still out on the deck. Hardy is leaning on ringside, looking
into the camera and showing plenty of weariness. Fade out.
Next day, we're sitting on a park bench, looking miserable. A
guy passing us (played by Eugene Pallette) is an insurance
agent and he suggests to Hardy that he should take out an
insurance policy on me as I am very likely to get hurt and
that means money in the bank. It's a cut-rate insurance
company he owns. The company gives $500 at a two-buck
fee for a single broken leg or arm. Hardy borrows the two
dollars from *me* and pays up (Hardy has taken the guy aside
so I can't hear any of this). Hardy then takes me for a walk
around town trying various methods to get me in an accident. He walks me under ladders where construction is going
on, and he gets conked instead. He passes a fruit stand and
buys a banana. As we are walking along, he peels it and
throws the skin in front of me so that I'll slip on it. I
unknowingly step over it. He picks it up, drops it in back of
him, and leads me around to walk on it again—and, of
course, he slips on it and crashes to the ground.

"We come to a bakery shop with a pie wagon standing in
front. Hardy drops the peel for me on the sidewalk there,
and the pieman comes along with a big tray of pies, and slips
on the peel. He's covered with pies. As he clears his eyes, he
happens to see Hardy pushing the banana into my hand, and
realizes that Hardy is trying to put the blame on me. An
argument starts, ending up with the pieman pushing a pie in
Hardy's face. I resent this and push a pie in the *pieman's*
face. Hardy laughs at this and the guy instead of hitting me
back hits Hardy with another pie. At this point, a stranger
passing by tries to stop the argument, and gets the pie in the
face, too. Gradually, one by one, other people get into the
argument until finally the entire street, a full block, is pie-
crazy. Everybody is pie-throwing happy. The camera goes up
to take a panorama view of all these people throwing,
throwing, throwing. There are pies thrown into a dentist's
office, in windows, out of them. Nothing but pies—thousands
of them. Then a cop who, of course, is all covered with pie
arrests us and is taking us away, but *he* slips on the banana
peel—and he falls down a manhole for the finish."

That, as nearly as words can do it, gives a very full picture
of *The Battle of the Century*. It is one of the great comedy

films of all time, and today it leads a lonely life in the vaults
of the Hal Roach studio.*

The Battle of the Century, like most of the early Laurel
and Hardy films, was made without worry about the pres-
sures of schedule. "We had a rough idea of schedule," Stan
points out, "but our prime worry was whether or not the
picture was going to be good. The studio didn't bother us
much if at all about a schedule because we didn't have a lot
of people in our casts as a rule. There weren't any unions,
and people just worked until we got the effects we wanted.
Sometimes we would have a change in a gag situation that
called for alteration of the set. So we'd wait a couple of days
until it was rebuilt. That takes time. We really didn't have
any idea of how precisely long it would take us to do a film.
It really depended on the kind we were doing. If we were
doing both day and night exterior shots on the same set we
would sometimes keep going right through the day and then
on all that night until the following morning. This, of course,
was when we felt like going ahead on a spurt to finish the
picture. It got pretty rough at times especially if we were
making water scenes. You can get pretty tired working all
night soaking wet as we did on many occasions. As for the
times between pictures, that always varied. After the picture
was assembled, we previewed it and if no retakes were
needed, we started to prepare the next story. That would
generally take three or four weeks, sometimes more, sometimes less. Years later, more time was taken on the feature
films, of course. If Roach was anxious for us to get started,
we'd go into production almost right away after finishing a
picture, and complete the script as we went along. We would
start out with an idea, go along working on it as we were
shooting, and then we would frequently deviate from the
original idea. We worked hard, but there was no real pres-
sure. It was fun, particularly in the silent days. If something
went wrong with what we were doing, we'd just 'cut' and
laugh about it. Then we'd talk it over and go on shooting. It
was damned fine fun and damned hard work in those days
when we were making ourselves a well-known team. Come to
think of it, it was always fun."

By 1928, the team of Laurel and Hardy was a *fait accom-
pli*. It was never to break up.

---

*A tantalizingly brief excerpt from *The Battle of the Century* was
seen in a comedy film history short, *The Golden Age of Comedy*
(1958).

Chapter V

THE SILENT SHORTS

"We had fun, and we did a lot of crazy things in our pictures," Babe Hardy was fond of saying, "but we were always real. Even when we did our shortest pictures, we tried to be real."

This is a truism of all great film comedy. The one- and two-reel film, like the one-act play, is not a dramatic vehicle that allows for a wide range of human activity, and yet emphatic identification by the audience of *human* characters in a *human* story is necessary for the true dramatic form. This is as true of comedy as it is of tragedy. Comedy and tragedy exist only in terms of human conduct. Clearly, there are delimitations of time and space imposed on the maker of the short film subject—delimitations that he must control and, if possible, turn to his advantage. He finds, initially, that there is just not enough room or full character development and full plot development simultaneously. One must go.

In examining the best comic films done from, say, 1910 through 1930, one receives the strong impression that the most successful of these ultimately are those that eschew plot and gags-for-gags-sake to concentrate on characterization—to concentrate as much as is possible on gags and incidents stemming from the foibles of human conduct. A thing perhaps not usually accorded to the most successful men in these comedies is that they all had magnificent acting ability. Buster Keaton, Charlie Chaplin, Harry Langdon, Fatty Arbuckle, and W. C. Fields were excellent actors. Had they worked in the classical theater, one can see them playing the great comedy roles. Chaplin with his savage dash would have romped deliciously through Molière, and Keaton as Bob Acres in *The Rivals* could have made the role his special property. And there is a clear parallel existing between the dim-witted zany of Shakespeare's *Twelfth Night,* Sir Andrew Aguecheek, and Stan Laurel. Indeed, when Alec Guinness played Sir Andrew at the Old Vic in London he deliberately emphasized this similarity: the jogging walk, the raised eyebrows, and the utterly vacuous smile. It was not an innovation: Shakespeare came home.

But the film comedians of the twenties and thirties did not have the world's best script writers to give them their roles; they had to lean on their own abilities to create good parts. They had usually acquired either through the English music hall or American vaudeville a solid sense of what was funny. They had used, reused, tried, and rejected gags of all varieties whatever. They came to the films knowing what was funny, and before the penetrating eye of the camera they were called on to create their own stories and their own characters. These characters had to have some kind of stability. An audience does not really remember a performer and his humor with affection until it knows or thinks it knows the performer. All lasting humor has a basic ingredient of audience identification with the thing being done and the person doing it. The audience must learn to know, remember and, ultimately, to love the comedian's form.

Had Laurel and Hardy been satisfied merely to think of themselves as gagsters, they could not have lasted. Where are the gagsters simon-pure of yesteryear? Comedians like Snub Pollard and Billy West were popular in their day, and seeing their films again causes one to marvel at their physical dexterity—their keen sense of elemental gag-making—but that is all. If one looks at two or three of their films, one has seen all. The mannerisms are trotted out and are laughable, but they do not persist in the memory because they are on the surface, not revelations of comic character. The pathos of Chaplin has perhaps been too much written about and possibly too much emphasized as being essential to his comedy equipment, but it is there and here and then and now in all of us, and that makes it appealing and perpetual.

An obvious criticism can be leveled at Laurel and Hardy in that they have a permanent sample-case of tricks which they use over and over again. Three of them already examined, the tie-twiddle, the camera look, and the cry certainly have been used continually in their films over the wide range of the years. Yet, these mannerisms come *out* of the screen characters of Laurel and Hardy. They are not superimposed. It would seem best, then, to determine what the characters of Laurel and Hardy are as they appear in the films.

The characters, like the team, were not created full blown. The two comedians never sat down to have a good, long chat about their "characters." There was no full consciousness of the process of creation of the two supremely silly and ignorant men identified in the films as Stan and Ollie. And yet theirs was an act of creation, or perhaps more accurately, theirs was a procedure of creative evolution.

These years of creation came during the late twenties and early thirties when they were concentrating in the short subject form of two- or three-reelers. At first, there was no conscious effort to wear a certain kind of costume. The derbies came early during the period of the silent shorts. Babe Hardy had been wearing a derby for comic effect since 1914 without any idea that it was an imitation of anyone. (Someone told him at the height of his success that it might in part be attributed to the fact that he and Stan had "copied" Chaplin's use of the derby.) Stan says, "The derby hat to me has always seemed to be part of a comic's make-up for as far back as I can remember. I'm sure that's why Charlie wore one. Most of the comics we saw as boys wore them, so I guess you'd say that's one item that's strictly in the public domain."

The Laurel and Hardy costuming was not of the strongly eccentric variety used to get a laugh for its own sake. "We never tried to use funny clothing," Stan points out. "Of course, there were times when we would wear odd garments for a special humorous effect, but as far as our two characters were concerned, we never tried to get very far from what was real. We always wore a stand-up collar but there wasn't anything unreal about them, especially in the twenties and early thirties. Stand-up collars were formal and slightly different but never too obviously so. They gave us, together with our derbies, a something we felt these two characters needed—a kind of phony dignity. There's nothing funnier than a guy being dignified *and* dumb. As far as make-up goes, I emphasized my lack of brains by making my face as blank as possible. I used very light make-up and made my eyes smaller by lining the inner lids. Babe, in keeping with his wish to obtain an even *bigger* kind of dignity, combed his hair down in a spit-curl bangs effect. This was in perfect harmony with his elegant nature and those fancy-dan gestures of his."

An unimportant 1927 two-reel picture, the title of which Stan cannot now recall, was significant in that it contributed to his permanent appearance as The Dimwit, and it was also to give him a gesture that became standard. Since the film was to concern the boys as convicts, he obligingly shaved his head down to a crew cut. Shortly after the completion of the picture when his hair was beginning to grow in, Stan removed his hat one day on the lot and tried to brush his hair back. It would not stay brushed. Some friends laughed at his ridiculous appearance, and laughter being the substance Stan Laurel's soul feeds on, the upraised hair became standard equipment from that moment on. It gave him, in effect, a natural fright wig—a sure laugh-getter since Aristophanes. He strengthened this appearance by a gesture of scratching his head and pulling up the hair simultaneously. The raised hair in turn emphasized his lean features and triangular chin thus making him the stuff of which brilliant caricatures are made.

These quotients of identity together with their devotion to the business of making comedy had entrenched them at the Roach Studies by 1928 as sure money-getters. The public began to take notice, and *The Film Exhibitor's Herald* saw that

> The transfer of Stan Laurel and Oliver Hardy from the All Star Series to a series to be known as the Laurel and Hardy Series is a perfectly logical one inasmuch as they proved during the current year that their personalities completely overshadow any descriptive title which otherwise might be given their comedies. Their success during the 1927-28 season has been outstanding.

The words "their personalities" are to be noted. They were emerging from the cocoon of the laugh factory into the open air of recognition as individuals. Thus was success begun, but success to be maintained depended on a number of important factors, not the least important of which was the quality of the studio gag men. There were no writers as such (except H. M. "Beanie" Walker who wrote the screen titles, a profession demanding wit and wit's soul, brevity), and gag men with literary backgrounds found themselves in practically a wordless world. The big need was for ideas. The idea men on the Roach lot were classified literally as gag men, and story conferences were really bull sessions in which the gag men would sit with Stan and the director to weave out the semblance of a plot for Laurel and Hardy. Babe was rarely at these sessions, not having great interest in the preparation of a script. From time to time he would suggest an idea, usually on the set, and it would be an excellent one, but the call of the golf course was clear.*

Sometimes the idea for a film would come from an object. One gag man happened to be passing a partially constructed house on his way to work. He brought a few thoughts to the gag session and a general working script was fashioned out of the discussion that followed. "Beanie" Walker, who later wrote much of the dialogue for the sound films, began to conceive the titles. Titles were held to a minimum. It has always been the mark of a good silent film when titles are sparse. One need only recall most of Chaplin's work or Fred Murnau's great film *The Last Laugh* to realize that one can, with imagination and talent, *show* the story instead of forcing the audience to read a significant amount of it. *The Finishing Touch* (1927) was the house-construction film, and the boys in trying to complete the partially built home ultimately demolish it.

Another Roach gag man found a starting point for a picture by watching a group of musicians playing in a nearby band shell. From this came *You're Darn Tootin'* (1928), directed by Edgar Kennedy of slow-burn fame. Featuring Laurel and Hardy as bandsmen, the film gave them an opportunity to thoroughly confuse and antagonize a prominent guest conductor. The ringing of changes on gags relating to rehearsal and performance is the heart of the picture, ending in inevitable chaos and disruption.

But the Roach gag men were not averse to following industry trends in their search for material. The late twenties saw a large output of domestic comedies in the total Hollywood product. It was a period in which the yet undefined theory of Momism was evidencing itself in many major features as well as short subjects. *Their Purple Moment* (1928), directed by Jimmy Parrott, brother of another Roach comic, Charley Chase, delineated the troubles of the boys in their continuing endeavor to get away from their domineering, Mom-like wives. This theme was to be used again and again in Laurel and Hardy films because it offered the ultimate contrast: two very stupid husbands trying to

---

* Charley Rogers tells of a practical way in which Stan harnessed Babe's love of golf for excellent use in the creation of the films. Rogers recalls, "At times Stan would deliberately hold off shooting the 'camera looks' until the end of the shooting day at a point when Babe would be dying to get out on the course. The result is that some of those exasperated looks you see Babe give are *really* exasperated looks!"

outwit two crafty and shrewish wives. Such a theme is not
new, and its success depends on implementing the basic
contrarieties. *Their Purple Moment* seen today is not anywhere near as funny as its stepchild, *Sons of the Desert,* a
Laurel and Hardy sound feature made years later which had
much more footage in which to establish the characters of
the wives. Nevertheless, the silent short contains authentic
comedy. Stan and Ollie (henceforth in these pages Hardy
on-screen is Ollie, Hardy off-screen is Babe) manage to sneak
out, and in the first flurry of exuberant freedom, find themselves innocently involved with two floozies in a night club.
The night club is featuring a midget troupe, singers and
dancers, who constitute the floor show. All goes well as the
quartet of merrymakers spin away their evening. It must
needs be that the wives show up and Stan and Ollie scoot
away to the kitchen where a wildly hilarious pie-throwing
episode erupts—so fast that it takes on the dimensions of a
chase finish." The chase—toujours the chase.

It is perhaps easy to think of the chase sequence as the
easy way out in ending a film. In the case of the one- or
two-reeler, however, it was in most instances mandatory.
Mack Sennett and Larry Semon were the great exponents of
the chase, but there is hardly a film of the golden days of
comedy that does not use the spirit of the chase in some
form or other in its final footage. In these early days of their
character development, Laurel and Hardy used the chase
frequently. It was then what it is now: a wrap-up, a gather-
ing of climaxes, and those who think that it is old-fashioned
need look back just a very few years to the magnificent
automobile chase used by W. C. Fields to end his memorable
The Bank Dick.

As the plotting and shooting of their films progressed
during 1928, it became apparent at the studio that Stan had
begun to take an active hand in the suggesting and working
out of gags, work not covered by his paycheck but work that
to him was not work. Although he never actually directed
any of the films, he was the director's strong right arm and,
in a few instances, both arms. He never intruded himself, his
suggestions were literally that, but everyone at the studio
behind camera knew the value of those suggestions. The
rapport between Stan and his directors was always a marked
one, and it was a gain added to gain that they happened to
be good friends as well.

One such, Clyde Bruckman, had been for some years a
hard-working director on the lot. He directed *The Battle of*

the Century and was well aware what was to be gained from active co-operation with Stan. (Bruckman later went on and made the very successful films *Feet First* and *Movie Crazy* with Harold Lloyd.) In 1928, Bruckman directed another early Laurel and Hardy masterpiece, *Leave 'Em Laughing,* a tour de force built, like so many of the films, around a very few simple and human gags.

For some time Stan had become aware of the need for pace in the creation of the comedy film. The tradition that comedy had to be fast to be good was one that persisted for many years. Even as late as the mid-thirties, the Marx Brothers, with their genius for insanity and shrewd in the knowledge of what makes people laugh, did not fully understand change of pace. *Duck Soup* and *Animal Crackers,* two of their typical early films and perhaps the best of them, are magnificently funny but woefully lacking in pace. The gags, almost all of them hilarious, come at such a rapid pace that one laugh frequently wipes out another. In the theater, an actor learns how to "hold." When he gets a laugh, he does not begin to speak his next line until the laughter dies. At times a laugh can last for ten, fifteen or more seconds. If the actor "walks through" his laugh, if he speaks during it, he may have unwittingly killed the good reaction that could have come on his next speech. The Marx Brothers were aware of this in the theater but when they began to make films they had no audience whereby to gauge reactions. It is possibly an apocryphal story that Irving Thalberg once enraged the Marx Brothers by suggesting that they needed someone to tell them about film comedy. If indeed it was he who told them of pacing, they presumably are grateful; their later films for M-G-M all show a much more restrained spacing of gags and the humor comes to the audience in fuller measure.

Stan Laurel was very much concerned with the problem. He had done quite a few films before his day as a star and it had always been his feeling that his earlier directors took the pictures along at too great a speed. He discussed the idea of "holding" with Bruckman and other directors. From their new restrained technique came pictures like *Leave 'Em Laughing.* Its excellence is all the more apparent when one compares it to other comedy films made in 1928. Stan felt strongly that the galloping cross-cutting of Sennett and early Roach was not the proper technique for two actors playing the roles of chuckleheaded fools. A booby usually needs time to make up what there is of his mind in order to react. Babe

Hardy had by this time made the camera look a standard part of his equipment. Here, then, was a perfect way to achieve a point of rest. At a moment when Stan does something incredibly stupid, something warranted to get a laugh, Ollie stops the action, looks in the camera and reacts. The audience laughs both at the stupidity and the reaction, and almost magically in the film house, the action does not begin again until the laugh is over. There was nothing accidental about this. When *Leave 'Em Laughing* was finished, Stan and various gag men sneak-previewed the picture a number of times and clocked the laughs. After an average of clocked laughs had been obtained, the picture went back to the studio and the "holds" (usually consisting of Ollie's camera looks) were either extended or diminished. In this way, the film was tailored exactly to an average audience, and not a single laugh was wasted. Stan, too, could create his own "hold" to a gag of Babe's by ungluing his eyes a few times in gradually dawning surprise until comprehension of the gag reached his minuscule brain.

The fascinating thing about *Leave 'Em Laughing* is that it is a half hour of hilarity built on only two gags: the antics of a man in a dentist's chair reacting to pain and laughing gas alternately, and a contretemps with a cop in a traffic jam.

The film reveals the boys' astounding ability to work up a simple gag to something rich and complex without ever deviating from its basic line. Listening to someone else laugh is not always a funny thing in itself; if, indeed, the laughter is prolonged and one is not in on the joke, the laughter is annoying. But when done with deliberate pace, such laughter can take an audience with it. In the early days of the gramophone, one of the most popular recordings ever sold was the famous "Laughing Record," a ten-inch disk which contained nothing but laughter. Perhaps that was a simpler age. However, in these days it is not uncommon to see a roomful of mature people listening to this old vintage record somewhat condescendingly and becoming progressively more and more amused by it until the hilarity in the room almost equals that of the record's. The secret of evoking this laughter, of course, is that the laughter on the record is controlled and paced. A slow giggle develops into a low titter. Diminuendo. The titter begins again somewhat tentatively and becomes a mild laugh. Laugh continues. Unexpectedly the laugh grows bigger and heartier, sinking occasionally into a fierce chuckle, from which it goes back to its old strength as a laugh. The laugh grows in volume and then explodes into a roar which amplifies into loud, loud, gasping wheezes of unrestrained delight. This, mind, is audible.

To be able to accomplish something like this in a silent film is little short of remarkable, but this is the accomplishment of *Leave 'Em Laughing*. First Stan and Ollie are accidentally subjected to the laughing gas. They laugh themselves out of the office, into the street, and from there, in their Tin Lizzie, out into traffic. They find themselves stopped in a jam which they have caused because of their inability to do anything else but laugh. An irascible cop, played by Edgar Kennedy, confronts them and is outraged by their silliness. The hilarity ranges far out, and the film ends as the entire street succumbs to paroxysms of pure delight. The laughter is a minor Niagara: it flows in cascading onrush.

"The funny thing about it to me now," Stan points out, "is that one time we actually had to stop shooting one day because we *were* laughing so much. I broke up Babe, and he broke me up. We finally had to call it a day when it got too much for us."

Particularly absorbing to watch in this film are the numerous variations of laughter employed: the subtle and sometimes not-so-subtle changes in facial expression, the unexpected writhings—above all, the controlled care the camera takes in building up a different form of laughter each time until a crescendo is reached and then carefully brought down again.

Laughter, measured or unmeasured, and beauty are irresistible in combination and Hal Roach was not ignorant of the practical uses of female loveliness in his pictures. Although he never extended himself to the point of having semiauthenticated bathing beauties like Sennett, he tried to use pretty girls whenever he could.

It is an interesting footnote to the history of these films that during the great period of the silent shorts, three very beautiful and talented girls made their screen debuts in them in preparation for fuller careers in later years. Paulette Goddard did a few bits in the films; Lupe Velez appeared in *Why Girls Love Sailors*; and the haunting Jean Harlow was the focus of one of the principal gags in *Double Whoopee* (1929).

Fascinating and saddening, too, is that two of these girls from the silent Laurel and Hardy films, and a third girl who acted with them when sound came, were to end their lives in tragedy. The proximity of comedy to tragedy has been cited frequently but never more pathetically than in the cases of

Lupe Velez, Jean Harlow, and Thelma Todd. All were beautiful, all were extremely competent comediennes and all died at the height of their careers. Lupe Velez killed herself and her unborn child when rejected by her lover; Jean Harlow (née Harlean Carpenter) died of uremia brought on by sun exposure at a time when the sorrow of her tragically unhappy marriage to Paul Bern was about to be lifted by her engagement to William Powell; and Thelma Todd was either killed or self-destroyed by carbon monoxide in her automobile, a victim, some say, of gangsters who had intruded themselves into her private life.

The Jean Harlow of *Double Whoopee* is a beautiful taffy-haired goddess of seventeen, remote from tragedy, one would say, by a multitude of light years. Her contribution to the film is not extensive. Ollie, as a splendidly caparisoned hotel doorman, swings to her cab and opens it with a large flourish and escorts her into the lobby. Stan, as carriage starter, has inadvertently closed the cab door on her gown and the entire back half of it is pulled away. A tracking shot follows her and Ollie as he conducts her with easy grace across the lobby. She is the picture of haughty beauty, totally unaware that her lovely legs are revealed.

Double Whoopee contains two Laurel and Hardy trademarks that were to stay with them for all their lives in the film. They are simple things, like all their trademarks, but they are oddly endearing. The first is the you-after-me-Stanley mannerism which Ollie always employs when entering or leaving a room. In Ollie's simple-minded view of the world, he must come first because he is the biggest; by nature, he feels, he must be the aggressive one. That his insistence on this arrangement invariably leads him into disaster is beside the point: he *must* come first. Stan accepts it quietly, and if Ollie cannot learn his lesson that taking the lead has its many dangers, Stan, too, cannot learn the corollary that he who takes the vanguard in the Laurel and Hardy world must inevitably bear the brunt of battle. But Stan never tires of trying to enter first.

The second trademark is Ollie's superb use of any writing instrument. In this film, the hotel manager, in the belief that this formidable person must surely be the eagerly awaited Grand Duke, conducts Ollie to the registration desk. Ollie removes his gloves ceremoniously, takes pen in hand and after three or four rococo curlicues in the air, signs his name with a flourish truly Napoleonic, pauses, lifts the pen lightly for a moment, and then thrusts the nib down sharply to make

a period indelible through eternity. The gentle humor in all
of this is something akin to that of the sight of an elephant
wearing lace panties. It is ridiculous on the face of it but,
possibly, only on the face of it. Is the world's way the only
way? Ollie's way is not our way but there is something in it
that attracts us essentially. Wouldn't we—don't we—enjoy
signing our name as he does but also do we not lose when we
hold back from signing our names as fully as he does—with
fervor, with panache, with joy?

Lewis R. Foster directed *Double Whoopee* from a basic
story dreamed up by Leo McCarey who had been acting as
Roach's assistant. McCarey frequently served as a starting
point for ideas. With his fine Irish mind easily attuned to the
possibilities of frenzy, he proved a natural idea man for
Laurel and Hardy. After some early directing, he had turred
more and more to writing and directing. (He was aided in
some of the early Laurel and Hardy films by a cameraman
named George Stevens.) The Lewis Foster-Leo McCarey
team was responsible for a 1929 release that, like so many
others, started out with the slimmest of ideas and burgeoned
out into a small object classic. The film, *Angora Love,* began
with a single object as its theme and not a wholly pleasant
object at that, a goat.

"The picture really had no plot," Stan remembers. "Just
that goat—but we sure got a lot of footage out of him. I give
a piece of cookie to the goat and he wants more so he
follows us around. We try every conceivable way to get rid
of him, but no use. We hid—we walked backward—we
disguised ourselves. Nothing helped. We finally brought the
goat to our room because the word had spread around that
the goat had been stolen and we didn't want to be arrested as
goatnappers. The comedy in our room consisted mainly of
the goat eating the stuffing from the furniture and Babe's
pants among other things. We gave it a bath, went to bed
with it, had trouble with the landlord over it. Later, when
sound came, we did a version of the same idea but substi-
tuted a chimpanzee for the goat. That was *The Chimp,* one
of the liveliest comedies we've ever done."

A goat, a chimp, any object that bespeaks comedy to most
people, is grist for the comedian's mill, and Laurel and Hardy
were fortunate in possessing through the years what might be
termed a human comedy object, Jimmy Finlayson, a stooge
who was more than a stooge. Finlayson continued to loom
large in many of the films. Whenever a dour crusty villain
was needed, Fin was the man. In many ways, he represented

the harshness of the world that buffeted Stan and Ollie. Jimmy Finlayson, Stan Laurel, Oliver Hardy, and Edward Everett Horton—these men have been the screen's supreme masters of the double take. Fin was very proud of this ability and even invented a very special variation on it which he lovingly called the "double take and fade away." It is inadequately described verbally but, in essence, it was a simple double take embellished by wide circular twistings of the head, concluding with the head thrown back violently as the right eye closed in a scornful squint and the left eyebrow rises impossibly high.

In *Big Business* (1929),* Finlayson had the chance to give what was perhaps his most superb double take and fade away. This film, again slim of plot, had the boys selling Christmas trees from door-to-door in mid-summer. As initially plotted, the comedy was to be worked out in such a fashion that various incidents would occur in various doorways—a series of short vignettes in slapstick. However, director James W. Horne and the gag men discovered that the second call, at Finlayson's house, afforded enough laughs for the entire two reels. In setting up the picture as happened on many occasions, it was thought that renting an actual home would be more realistic and more practical than building a set. (This proved to be a bit of a drawback because the gags created almost obliterated the house from its lot.) At one point when Finlayson was talking with the boys in his doorway, the opportunity came for a magnificent take. "Lemme go, boys! Stand back, men!" he told the crew, and then as the cameras started to whirr, he went into what he meant to be his most spectacular fade-away ever. It was. On the snapback his head struck the brick portal of the doorway knocking him cold—a notable example of giving one's all for one's art.

That year—1929—was a year of disruption for filmmakers as for us all. The market crash did not affect business markedly on the Roach lot, but people in the company suffered personal losses. Stan was one. "There was a period there," he says, "when several of the banks closed and I lost $30,000. Later I recovered five or six thousand of it. It was because of this loss that I invested in annuities and thank God I did. I would be without a decent income at the present time. Like everybody else, I was interested in making money. This stems from my vaudeville days when I was making very little of it. When I was on what we used to call the 'small time,' $250 a week was tops. It was really a struggle in vaudeville. When you were out on the road, you had to make big jumps from city to city, and out of that salary we also had to pay agent's commission, living expenses, baggage transfer, and tips to the stage crew. On top of that, we had to do things like keeping up a decent wardrobe and furnishing pictures for lobby display. Many times we only played split weeks and sometimes none at all, or we'd pick up a Saturday or Sunday date for twenty-five or thirty bucks.

"In pictures if a comic was lucky enough to get a contract for a series—I'm speaking of the early days now—his contract stayed at $250 a week for the first year and a raise each year for the remainder of the contract which was usually of five years' duration. But there really wasn't any fixed price for comics. They were a dime a dozen in those days and they were happy to work in pictures for anything they could get. Even Chaplin started at $125 a week, and then of course his sudden popularity put him in a position to write his own ticket."

During most of the depression period, Hal Roach Pictures were released by Metro-Goldwyn-Mayer, and Laurel and Hardy were frequently featured in M-G-M advertisements. In 1929, when the transition to sound was under way, M-G-M wanted to announce its debut in sound and to do so put all its contract players of note into a single film. The result, a wildly mixed affair, was *The Hollywood Revue of 1929,* one of the first "all-star" films. The entire starring stable of M-G-M was trotted out, and Laurel and Hardy came along to furnish some comedy. The film cannot be shown today unless M-G-M re-releases it with a film sound track. Available prints offer the sound only on disks. The Laurel and Hardy contribution was limited by lack of a set, rehearsal time, and a plot, but in characteristic fashion, they did much with little and turned up something that might well have played effectively on vaudeville stages of the time. Ollie was featured as a magician and Stan complicates and finally ruins the act by revealing the tricks. Ollie is continually discomfited by Stan's ingenuousness and ultimately gets his face shoved into a white, gooey cake. In trying to shove the cake back into Stan's face, he inadvertently throws it into the face of Jack Benny, master of ceremonies. This was not their native humor and only faintly amusing slapstick results. *The Holly-wood Revue of 1929,* whatever else it might have been, was a sign of the times. Sound was here, and with it an ominous note: silent comedians could be silent no longer.

Chapter VI

THE SOUND SHORTS

In the Hollywood of the late twenties, sound became both bogy and blessing. Those who failed did so resoundingly; those with top marks attained an even stronger grip on the affections of the public. The classic example of the failure was John Gilbert, but what is sometimes not remembered is that there was absolutely nothing wrong with his voice. Anyone who saw him in *Queen Christina* with Garbo in the mid-thirties will recall that his tones were persuasively masculine and quite in keeping with his fabled personality. What hit Gilbert and others like him was the industry's misuse of sound through overemphasis and imperfect means of reproduction. The movies of a sudden could talk; the difficulty was that they did nothing but talk, and too frequently the talk was squeaky.

It would not be quite accurate to say that Laurel and Hardy ignored sound. They gave it a friendly and respectful nod and went about their business. Babe Hardy and Stan Laurel had not used their voices for comic purposes before paying audiences for some years. The gentle, warm, Southern Hardy tenor and Stan Laurel's soft Lancashire speech were distinctive and pleasant on the sound track. (Especially distinctive were Babe's Georgia-gentleman pronunciation of boid for bird, woid for word, and Stan's North Country first syllable emphasis of words, *con*-trol, *con*-dition.) They made the transition to sound easily. There is hardly any difference between their last silent two-reelers and their early sound two-reelers. Sound is there but it is an adjunct, not a master. Some silent comedians felt that with sound the prime duty was now to tell stories in words. Laurel and Hardy, fortified with the knowledge that in the cinema the visual takes precedence over the audial as opposed to the reverse rule in the theater, went ahead in the same well-sweetened way. They utilized sound; they were not ruled by it.

An exceptionally good use of it is seen in their first talkie, *Unaccustomed As We Are* (1929). Directed by Lewis Foster, the film featured the energetic and steel-voiced Mae Busch who later achieved a negative fame in Jackie Gleason's television shows of the 1954-55 period with their constant references to "the ever popular Mae Busch," a symbol to modern audiences of the old film days. Mae, a dynamic comedienne, was the epitome of the harsh-tongued, shrewish wife in most of the Laurel and Hardy films in which she appeared. In *Unaccustomed As We Are* she walks out on her husband Ollie when he brings Stan home to dinner. Next door, a cop's wife (Thelma Todd) hears of the boys' dilemma and volunteers to cook for them. In a mishap, her dress is burned and she is forced to hide in a trunk when Mae and the cop (who had to be and was Edgar Kennedy) appear on the scene. Kennedy discovers that the trunk contains feminity of some sort and he gleefully insists that the boys bring the trunk over to his apartment. This done, Thelma rises from the trunk and confronts her husband by breaking all the furniture over his head. (This story was used as a part of the full-length *Blockheads* nine years later.)

Sound in *Unaccustomed As We Are* is mostly of the routine sound-effect variety but there is one excellent and imaginative use of it that was to point the way for many future comedy makers. Combined with a basic principle of editing, it later became a cliché. Stan, in informally supervising the film, was faced with a common, kitchen-variety gag, a tumble downstairs. This device was as basic to comedy films as the prat-fall or the slide on the banana. Stan thought of treating this action in a new way, a way specifically geared to the sound film. Stan appeared at the top of the stair, stumbled, reacted with horror and fell out of sight as the camera remained focused on the top of the stair. Ollie appeared, reacting with a wince as the camera stayed with him. Then the sound track does its work giving forth with a gigantic and prolonged crash. As common (indeed as overworked) as this seems to us today, it was a complete innovation then.

Stan explains his feelings about it at the time: "I thought then that there was nothing really funny about a guy falling downstairs. There's pain connected with it and that's never funny. I realized, of course, that you can take away the sting by not having the man really hurt, but there's nothing real about that. In that scene we *removed* the pain by having the camera stay looking at the top of the staircase. The sound effect of the fall lets the audience visualize its own scene, and that just made it funnier to them." This use of suggestive visualization became a part of Laurel and Hardy technique but like all their techniques, it never became obtrusive.

In their representations of an uncommon variety of the common man, Laurel and Hardy have been everything from tramps to businessmen to convicts to detectives, and inevitably to sailors and soldiers. It was as sailors that they did *Men o' War* (1929), one of their sunniest comedies. In fact, the sun was dominant throughout the film and it combines with the boys' white ducks and the light, sure touch of their comedy to create a luminous picture of two simple, lighthearted gobs, pure of heart and manner, out for a holiday in the spring of all the world. They come with their larcenous-hearted girls to an amusement park by a lake. With fifteen cents between them, the ever-knowledgeable Ollie has a perfect plan to circumvent any heavy expenditure. "Now, look, Stanley," he says, "we've got just enough money for three glasses of soda pop. I'll ask the girls what they want, I'll take sarsaparilla, and when I ask you what you want, you say, 'I don't want anything, thank you.' OK?" "Sure," says Stan.

With vast ceremony and a manner implying that he is asking if they prefer black or gray caviar, Ollie determines the girls' taste in soda and adds his order to it. Then as an afterthought he says politely to Stan: "And what will you have, Stanley?" Stan thinks for a moment and then says sedately, "I'll have sarsaparilla too, thank you." Camera look by Ollie and a frantic conference with Ollie on the side to repeat instructions. The ceremonial is repeated: "And what will *you* have, Stan?" Much cogitation on Stan's part but he brightens and says, "I'll *still* have sarsaparilla, thank you." Ollie's disgust threatens to overwhelm them all when one of the floozies says to him, "Oh, general, don't be a piker. Give him what he wants." With teeth grating, Ollie inquires of Stan a third time, confident that the message has finally penetrated. Again, hard thinking on Stan's part and he comes up triumphantly with the statement that he really doesn't want any soda pop, he wants a banana split instead. Ollie slaps him and Stan retaliates by sticking his fingers in Ollie's eyes. (Whenever the boys fight it lasts for the duration of the lighting of a cigarette.) Ollie orders for the girls and then tie-twiddles coyly to the tough-looking counterman (who could it be but Finlayson?) and announces that "my friend and I will have *a* glass of sassafras, please." A moderate take from Finlayson, who brings the drinks. Stan is permitted to drink his half first. He puts his straw in the glass and drinks it all. Ollie heaves a mammoth sigh at this and stares at the camera. He asks Stan, "Now, *why* did you do that?" Stan cries and gulps out, "I couldn't help it. My half was on the *bottom!*" This is not the end of Ollie's troubles. He calls for the check with great confidence and is appalled to discover that the bill is thirty, rather than fifteen cents. He gives the bill to Stan who, accidentally hitting the pin ball machine, hits the jackpot, winning a reserve of cash.

The boys rent a rowboat and Ollie sits in the back with the two girls as Stan rows. Stan can only make the boat go in a circle and Ollie impatiently grabs up and puts in his oar. Both row in the same direction, then realizing that they should reverse, they switch simultaneously, thus causing the boat to increase its speedy circling. As they fight each other for the oars, the camera does a cross-cut to Finlayson, "taking" and mugging horrendously on the bank. A canoeist comes along-side and calls them a pair of dumbbells.

Then, in a wildly cascading series of catastrophes: Stan sloshes a hat full of water at the interloper; interloper throws water at Ollie; Ollie hits interloper with paddle; interloper hits Stan; Ollie breaks interloper's paddle; interloper gets knocked in the water; interloper crawls into the boys' boat to fight; Ollie throws cushion accidentally at another boat which capsizes it; third boat runs to help the capsized boat; *this* boat is capsized by rocking; all the people in the water climb into the boys' boat; two policemen and Finlayson come along in still another boat, are promptly capsized and join the mob in the Laurel and Hardy boat. Everyone—thirteen people—is engaged in a wild cushion fight and the film ends as the boat sinks slowly under the weight of the melee. This sequence is one that would have been rushed to death in the early days of film comedy. Here, although the action is swift, it is not overly so. The succession of events is inevitable, going from cause to cause, and it begins leisurely. The tempo increases by means of effective cross-cutting, and reaches utter mad-ness and full pitch (the madness and pitch that came on early in Sennett films) just a few seconds before the final fade. In *Men o' War*, the height of destruction is reciprocally at-tained, but in realistically paced progression.

In addition to its being another hilarious example of the reciprocal destruction device, another good film, *The Perfect Day* (1929) brought into being a use of sound that has since become commonplace in the cinema. This, again, came at a time when sound was not yet out of swaddling clothes. *The Film Exhibitor's Herald* reports with awe:

> In one spot Hardy hits Laurel over the head with an automobile jack and the noise from the blow sounded like the ringing of an anvil when struck with a twelve-pound hammer. It is the funniest sound effect yet recorded.

In later years, this too became a standard sound trick of the Warner Brothers' Bugs Bunny cartoons, and in turn was copied by Paul Terry for Terry Toons and by other animators.

In plotting *The Perfect Day*, it had been anticipated that the boys would appear at a picnic. Part of the footage was to show the mix-ups attendant on departure but the greater part of the film was to concern the picnic itself. However, as was to happen in a number of the films, the fun intended for the initial footage extended itself for the rest of the picture. The boys and their wives are preparing a picnic at Ollie's house. Included in their plans is Ollie's gouty and grouchy father-in-law (Edgar Kennedy) who sits hunched up over his bandaged foot, brandishing a cane to guard it from possible knocks. (We are, obviously, going to see more of that foot.) The boys enter beaming from the kitchen with a large platter of sandwiches they have prepared. Stan accidentally knocks the platter over Ollie who is inundated with sandwiches. Ollie, furious, bangs Stan over the head with the tray. Loud *b-o-o-o-inng* sound effect (another first). One of the wives insists that they make up and the camera pans to the two of them, side by side, terribly indignant. For a long minute they go through a mutual transition from deep anger to petulance to poutiness to bashfulness to a faint smile to coy looks at each other concluding with a big smile and a handshake. They are pals again and the sandwiches are tidied up.

Stan, smiling happily, proceeds into the kitchen in front of Ollie and accidentally allows the swinging door to hit the tray again and bring the mountain of sandwiches down on Ollie once more. A striking feature of the Stan-Ollie friendship is that despite double indignities such as this one, the deep warmth between the two was never broken up for any time beyond a minute. From film to film, they become estranged but only fleetingly. Ollie is usually the fall guy (most of the time quite literally) and if his anger is swift and terrible, the making-up process is equally swift—and pleasant. Ollie can never understand why Stan is so dumb and Stan can never understand why Ollie gets so indignant about something which, after all, is not *his* fault even though Ollie is glaring at him with head covered with water, oil, flour, tar, and/or molasses. Ollie glares and Stan, in innocent and uncomprehending discomfort at the sight of his anger, waves his hands in the air to cover his embarrassment or tries to fold his arms in front of him but his elbows give way weakly leaving him even more naked unto his enemies.

The merrymakers in *The Perfect Day* pile into the Tin Lizzie parked in front of the house and prepare to speed off. They wave good-by to neighbors across the street who wave back, shouting "Good-by, good-by!" Then the car will not start. Stan gets out to investigate and does some mysterious, incomprehensible things that help not at all. Kennedy's goutridden foot has been placed up over the side of the open car's rear door and one knows that it will get banged when the time comes. The time duly arrives and the banging is with a vengeance. Hitting a gouty foot will get a laugh; hitting it a second time will cut the laugh by half, and to hit it a third time might well bring audience resentment. It takes artistry to hit a gouty foot seven times within a few minutes and get good, solid laughs at each assay, and yet this is precisely what happens. Field work has been done here to document the laughs. At the Newsreel Cinema in Birmingham, England, in 1953, a test taken at a showing of *The Perfect Day* recorded seven full-bodied ten-second laughs for this one short sequence.

The sequence: Kennedy accidentally hits his own foot with his cane; Stan pulls a supporting chair away from the foot and it falls; a dog tugs at the foot; Stan slams the car door on the foot; Stan steps on the foot; Stan sits on the foot; when the car is jacked up, the car crashes down on it. "Now, this overdone or come tardy off . . ." said Hamlet, "cannot but make the judicious grieve." These are the exact pitfalls avoided by Stan Laurel in this action. The hitting of the gouty foot is never overdone; it is made on each occasion to seem a natural accident. They are spaced by means of good editing so that one is not expecting them and when they come, they are a result of purely natural movement. Nor are they "come tardy off." They come when they should come and this is determined in the cutting room. Stan Laurel frequently supervised the editing of his own films not because he did not trust the Roach editing staff but because he had a definite idea of the tempo needed for the comedy he wanted.

Excellent editing technique is also seen in the use of the neighbors on the porch across the street. The moment the Laurel and Hardy party settles down in the car ready to speed off, as noted, they exchange big waves and loud good-bys with the neighbors. This is repeated three times more throughout the film and serves as a sort of intermission or act-break to the action. We have gone through a set-piece of troubles and now, at last, we are ready to start off on our glorious ride into the country. "Good-by, good-by!" Each time the neighbors call, we feel that at last we are going to get away but, alas (or happily), we do not. One of the delays is caused by running over a nail. Another time the clutch is sticking and Ollie goes out to investigate as Stan climbs into the driver's seat. "Throw out the clutch, Stan," Ollie commands. Stan does, jettisoning the mechanism, and Ollie hurls it back at his head. "Good-by, good-by!" The motor starts but grinds down as smoke pours out. Stan rushes over to a neighbor, grabs the lawn hose and comes back, to drench Ollie accidentally. Ollie hurls the jack at Stan and it goes through the neighbor's window. It is the beginning of another scene of reciprocal destruction.

If the scene that follows were to be done at breakneck speed, it would be the Sennett hit-and-run all over again. Instead the action is deliberately slowed down for the purposes of laughs. One can laugh at reciprocal destruction done in quick anger but when it is done slowly with each victim taking his turn at punishment with angelic patience, the laughter is intensified. The neighbor, outraged at the broken window, does not run over to find revenge. He *saunters* over, picks up a brick on the way and carefully, slowly, tosses it through the car's windshield. Not showing a whit of anger, Stan takes a brick, walks over to the neighbor's house and breaks another window. The neighbor, while Stan and Ollie look on almost amiably, throws a brick through one of Ollie's house windows. At the precise moment when we have had enough of this, all participants blanch with horror at the sight of someone coming down the sidewalk off-camera and they disperse. The neighbor rushes home, the picnickers flee to Ollie's house. The camera tracks back for a view of Ollie's home and holds for three seconds before a parson strides unctuously by. He passes. The picnickers flock back to the car and pile in. "Good-by, good-by!" The car starts with a happy roar, picks up speed, turns at the corner and travels twelve feet before it reaches a street area under construction. The car descends slowly into an unmarked morass and muddy water covers all.

The Film Exhibitor's Herald, in an ecstatic review, exhorted managers to book the film and almost off-handedly concluded the story with two sentences which explain why Laurel and Hardy were able to make the transition from silent to sound pictures without a ripple on the water:

> Incidentally, pantomime is still their strongest weapon. They use dialogue as a kind of punctuation.

As 1930 began, Laurel and Hardy were recognized as major comedians. Roach had set up what he hoped would be an annual commitment to M-G-M of ten two-reelers, an arrangement smacking of the production-line concept. Nonetheless, despite some minor efforts strained in story and conception, the 1930 quota of films was generally excellent. One imaginative gag-men session brought a stimulating idea to the production of *Brats,* filmed that year. Acting under the assumption that the only thing funnier than Laurel and Hardy would be two Laurel and Hardys, the idea was born of having the boys play their own sons. The idea, which could have been oppressively cute, paid off. The studio, "sparing no expense," built conventional interior sets and then duplicated them in giant size. When the boys were playing themselves, they played on the regular set; when attired in Buster Browns as their sons, they gamboled on the large set. The excellent construction and attention to detail on the giant set gave reality to the film which would have been woefully lacking had it been anything else than very good. The idea that the film is a stunt does not actively break into the spectator's consciousness, and much of this is due to the believability of the boys as children. They are not adults acting as children; they *are* children. It is a clue to their screen personalities.

Up until 1930, Laurel and Hardy had not received attention from serious film critics. The trade journals were frequently perceptive in their reviews but much of their enthusiasm was stimulated by the fact that Laurel and Hardy were paying off at the box office. Exhibitors knew that business could be stepped up simply by billing them, names alone, above the featured picture. One of the first important critics to be attracted was Pare Lorentz. He noted the Laurel and Hardy pace with some surprise in *Judge*:

I am late getting around to Laurel and Hardy. I always suspect all clichés. I have never joined the Amos 'n' Andy school and I do not belong to the now deceased Moran and Mack league. However, without a doubt, the two-reel comedies of Laurel and Hardy are the best directed and funniest movies being made today. The director, James Parrott, has developed a peculiar, methodical, simple routine for his comedy team. The last one I saw, *Blotto,* had very few gags and not much story. But the gags were pulled so deliberately and with such finesse, I wonder that Mr. Parrott does not establish a new school of movie direction.

Lorentz had no way of knowing that Parrott, although an extremely able man, was only continuing a tradition of pacing that Stan Laurel had carefully built up almost instinctively. But Stan has always been very careful to insist on proper credit for the creation of the films. He says, "I don't by any means take credit for most of the comedy ideas since gags and routines were suggested by many of the gag men. I would take the one that appealed to me, and with their help, work it out to fit our characters. I certainly never directed the pictures, but I guess you might say that I sort of stood on the sidelines and helped."

That he did a bit more than help is attested to by Charley Rogers, who directed some of the greatest Laurel and Hardy films.

"Stan was the spirit behind the director," Rogers has said. "He never intruded himself, and there probably wouldn't have been any reason for him to intrude because all of us worked in real harmony. We were all friends, thank God, and that helped a lot. But whenever Stan suggested something in conference or during shooting, it almost always proved to be the right thing. He, perhaps more than anybody else, knew by instinct the kind of gags needed. He watched closely over the pictures, but it was like kind of a beneficent father, not a bossy one who always wanted his own way at any cost. You see, by nature he is a polite man and a gentle fellow, and those two qualities always came over, in front of the camera and behind it. He was the director's conscience. Everyone of us who worked on those pictures had a real *feeling* for those two lovable, silly characters before the camera, and we tried to remain as faithful as we could to the boys' conception of them. It's hard to explain what I mean by 'conception.' Stan and Ollie weren't really planned; they just grew. We all watched that growth and tried to help it along. And even that's hard to spell out for you—the growth, I mean. We knew *who* those two fellows were, but I don't think we ever stopped and talked about how they got that way. It's just this simple: they grew, just like kids grow."

Blotto, which moved Pare Lorentz over into the Laurel and Hardy camp, was in story line the same old thing. Based on the hoary theme of married men getting away from their wives, it duplicates basic incidents from their silent shorts, but the sense of characterization is much stronger. Laurel and Hardy stand-bys are seen again. The Tin Lizzie is there, as ever was. A number of Model T Fords served as standard props for a great number of the pictures. There was a full stable of them on the lot. Some were kept in almost completely wrecked condition to be used at the end of a disaster sequence; others were held together by baling wire in such a fashion that they could be picked apart, section by section. One of them was squeezed fore and aft into an accordion shape, and yet another was sliced precisely in half for an unusual comic effect. The Tin Lizzie, Stan, and Ollie made a companionable trio; they were all simple, uncomplicated, out of date in a swiftly moving world, and durable. *Blotto* ends with the aggressive Mrs. Laurel (Anita Garvin) blasting the boys' car into pieces. An old device, the shotgun-blast ending was a *deus-ex-machina* finish for many of the early films. This became too familiar a contrivance but in the semi-factory set-up that was the Roach studio at the time, *deus-ex-machinas* had to be part of standard procedures.

Certainly it was not easy to incorporate novelty at every turn when one is expected to complete ten two-reel films a year. This scheduling, not always maintained because of the creators' insistence on quality at almost any cost, nevertheless imposed on Stan and his co-workers the need to rely on several basic formulas. And a basic formula may well serve as a solid foundation for unusual creative effects when an actively creative comic mind is at work. A 1930 film, *Hog Wild*, shows Laurel and Hardy with the most fundamental of their formulas—the two of them confronting and being confronted by a simple object. Here they are at their finest, working on the thread of an idea and spinning infinite variations on it. As at all the times when they were at their creative best, they needed only one or two simple gags around which to build a very full two-reeler. In *Hog Wild*, the plot is contained in four words: putting up an aerial. Basil Wright, the brilliant documentary director, has vast

The gallant Ollie escorting a haughty Jean Harlow to the registration desk of a hotel in *Double Whoopee*.

Flirtatious gobs meet flirtatious girls. *Men O'War.*

A pair of potential beer barons prepare to purchase the artifacts of their profession. *Pardon Us.*

Stan and Ollie as they best enjoyed themselves —in period costume. *Fra Diavolo.*

Ollie in deep trouble at the mercy of a sleep-benumbed Stan. *Fra Diavolo.*

In *Brats*, they play their own children with total authenticity.

Set to lunge with total inexpertise at an imaginary enemy. *Bonnie Scotland.*

Ollie, with the inevitable, "Well, here's another fine mess you've gotten me into!" *Bonnie Scotland.*

A cat without his fiddle eyes Stan, to Ollie's bewilderment. *Babes in Toyland*.

They stare with fearful apprehension at absolutely nothing while the studio still photographer asks for one more. *Swiss Miss*.

The ape they inadvertently let plunge to the bottom of the rocky chasm in *Swiss Miss* returns to threaten them with flailing crutch.

In *Blockheads*, Stan demonstrates a bit of white magic—the igniting of
his thumb.

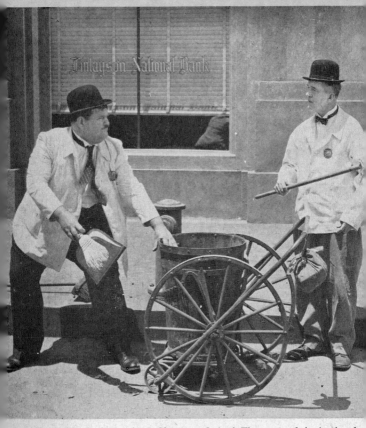

Following the horses in *A Chump at Oxford*. The name of the bank, of course, is an "in" joke.

Babe, Sir Harry Lauder, and Stan at the great Scots entertainer's home, Lauder Ha', Strathaven, Scotland.

Babe getting out of a car in midst of a crowd which surrounded them, Grantham, England, 1947, on tour. The crowds never diminished through the years.

Relaxing in depth by judging a bathing-beauty contest, Morecambe, England, 1947.

Rehearsing their song and dance for the 1947–48 tour, Alhambra Theatre, Brussels.

They were wise enough to know the kind of costume to wear when they
appeared in a Glasgow theater, 1947.

In Dublin, 1953, during rehearsals for the final tour of the British Isles.

Stan and Ida Laurel with Lucille and Babe Hardy during lifeboat drill on their return to the U. S. after the final tour, 1954.

affection for this film because of its richness of variation. He describes the climax:

> In this film, the attempt to fix a wireless aerial on the roof of Hardy's house precipitated Hardy off the roof into a goldfish pond at least five times. Each time a different gag-variation appeared, until the comedy passed into the realm of cutting, and the final fall was but a flight of birds and the sound of a mighty splash. Even Eisenstein would have been proud to do it.

This climactic shot was the product of the imagination of Stan Laurel whose close attention to the editing process was becoming more and more evident in the films. An editor can make or mar a picture. In putting together all the footage printed, he must arrange the sequence of action clearly, meaningfully, dramatically. By personally supervising the editing of his own films, Stan was easily able to remove the irrelevant and extraneous and arrange the gag variations so that they led to the proper climax.

In the same year *Hog Wild* was filmed, Hal Roach decided on an experiment which did little to advance the artistic standing of his most popular team. Metro-Goldwyn-Mayer, in showing off the talents of its bright new singing star from the Metropolitan Opera, Lawrence Tibbett, cast him in *The Rogue Song*, a romantic, on-the-Romany-trail adventure film. It was essentially a display case for Tibbett's singing, and in this respect the film is notable. In a typical Hollywood "cast insurance" move, M-G-M asked Roach for the loan of Laurel and Hardy. The film had already been made and previewed and it was decided to add comedy relief between some rather tired romantic situations. Moreover Tibbet was not a name overseas and Laurel and Hardy were now well-known in foreign markets. That Laurel and Hardy were particularly comic in the film or that relief was needed from Tibbett's splendid singing is debatable. Certainly Laurel and Hardy were not happy in this new situation. Removed from the S.O.P. of the Roach lot they were not so much fish out of water as fish in an overstocked barrel. They did not have their freedom to do their comedy as they wanted to, and to compound this, they were directed in their scenes by Lionel Barrymore who, despite his great talents as an actor, was not exactly an Academy Award prospect as a director. In the case of comedy he was totally inadequate. He had only the vaguest idea of the Laurel and Hardy technique, and after

some attempts at direction, he wisely left them alone to do
what they could with the dialogue and the situations that had
been written for them. These, to put it pleasantly, were
uninspired. The apogee of their comic efforts in the film
probably occurs when Ollie, at Stan's suggestion, uses a
barrel to mount his horse and plunges through the top into
water. The rest is silence. Of these efforts, *Outlook* magazine's film critic said tersely, "Faintly comic relief is furnished
by Laurel and Hardy." It was precise evaluation.

The years 1931 through 1933 were unquestionably the
most rewarding for Laurel and Hardy in the short-subject
field. During that time they made potboilers and remakes,
but they were also years of real accomplishment. Among the
1931 films, *Our Wife* offers a poignant footnote to film
comedy history because it was one of the few films made by
Ben Turpin in a come-back try. This hardy perennial of an
earlier day had retired from comedy years before to care for
an ailing wife. Playing a justice-of-the-peace whose comic
myopia causes difficulties in determining just who is being
married, Turpin's brief appearance in the film was amusing
but not of sufficient duration to give him a chance to sparkle.

One of the better films, *Helpmates* (1931), shows a
growth in the development of Stan and Ollie characters.
(Stan calls them simply "those two fellas.") *Helpmates,* as
per its title, has for its theme Stan helping Ollie to disaster
but more strongly than in any other film previously. The film
opens with a closeup of Ollie speaking sternly to someone:
"Now aren't you ashamed of yourself? What did you do? I'll
tell you. . . You took advantage of your wife's absence and
pulled a wild party. Could anything be more crass—more
disgusting? I'll tell you what's wrong with you in two words:
im—possible!" The camera tracks back to reveal Ollie talking
to himself in a mirror. The phone rings and Ollie demands of
his caller, Stan, "Where have you been?"

Stan says, "Why, I've been here—with me."

"And where were you last night?"

"I couldn't come to the party," Stan says, "because a dog
bit me."

"Bit you?"

"Yes," says Stan, "he bit me. B-i-*it* me. Bit me!"

"Where?" demands Ollie.

"Here!" says Stan, who carefully lowers the telephone to
show Ollie the injured area.

It is this straightforward imbecility that came to be the primary trademark of the Stan Laurel character. In the earliest films, Ollie and Stan are simply dumbbells; sometime during the early thirties, slowly, complete and profound and delightful stupidity gained ascendancy. That this is character development in the usual meaning of the phrase is, of course, nonsense, but it is a deepening of characteristics that had only been suggested by the first films. It is not possible to tell when this point of utter vacuousness in mentality was reached. It was, in the main, a matter of accretion of stupidity gags until Stan and the gag-men started to think continually of his character as having not a mote of sense. The same process applied to Ollie. His dumbness, too, increased until it reached profound proportions. In contrast to Stan, his courtly façade gave him an appearance of rationality, and yet he was possibly even more ignorant because he thought he was brighter. The absurdity of such lines in *Helpmates* as

OLLIE: You never met my wife, did you?
STAN: Yes, I never did.

helps define their difference. Such ignorance infuriates Ollie. He looks at the camera as if to say, "How can a man *be* so dumb?" and then in the next minute he does something equally imbecilic. Babe Hardy defined his character's own special brand of ignorance: "I'm the dumbest kind of guy there is. I'm the dumb guy who thinks he's smart."

Helpmates consists of a slowly rising crescendo of mishaps caused by assorted dumb tricks with Ollie receiving indignity upon indignity until one stupendous blow at the fadeout. Stan has inadvertently caused Ollie's house to blow up and burn. Ollie sits, crushed beyond retaliatory action, in the open-roofed shell of his house. "Well," Stan says in propitiating tones, "I guess there's nothing else I can do." "No," says Ollie, "I guess not." "Well, I'll be seeing you," Stan says hopefully. "Goodbye," Ollie answers quietly. Stan walks to the front door which is miraculously still standing. "Hey!" Ollie says, "would you mind closing the door? I'd like to be *alone*." There is a sudden gust of rain descending on Ollie as if to deal him fate's final blow. He carefully and tidily picks some lint off his suit, and looks heavily at the camera. He sighs. Slow fade.

In any analysis of screen humor, the use of drunkenness as

a laugh-getter has never been fully assessed, nor shall it be here. But in these days of more "mature" humor, drunkenness is not with us as it was. Obviously today nobody whoops it up anymore, but in the thirties people in films did get wildly drunk once in a while without hurting anyone but themselves. Chaplin's wild antics under the influence are still memorable, and they influenced a number of drunk scenes in many comedies of the twenties and thirties. Laurel and Hardy, too, used alcohol to stimulate laughs, and in their early films it was in the basic and somewhat crude fashion of the day. They would get drunk in a night club and do the amiably senseless things that drunks might do, adding their own brand of nonsense. But as their characters developed into the two benign and inherently sinless nincompoops, the liquor did not flow as much. Whenever they drank, it was always innocently done and drunkenness was always an accident. In *Scram* (1932), they are led into drunkenness because of the spirit of charity resident deep within them.

They have been ordered to get out of town by a perpetually scowling magistrate who hates vagrants and drunks with equal intensity. Since the boys fall into the first category only, they are lucky to receive one hour's grace to depart the town's limits. As they go into the driving night rain, they encounter a drunk (the perpetual souse of many comedy films, Arthur Housman), and try to help him find his house-keys which have slipped through a sidewalk grate. In the process of extrication, they suffer minor indignities and are eager to be up and away but the drunk insists on taking them to his home because they have no place to go. They have great trouble getting inside the house. The keys don't seem to fit. But once in through an open window, all goes most pleasantly. They are given a good room and silk pajamas to wear. The drunk thoughtfully leaves a water pitcher which the boys do not realize is filled with gin. In error, they stumble into a matronly lady's boudoir. She screams and faints and is revived with the gin.

Her fright softened by the spirits, she is calmed completely with the assurance that her husband has merely given the boys shelter for the night. She is not only calmed; eventually she is amused by the mistake. What follows is essentially the laughing-jag routine used in the silent film, *Leave 'Em Laughing*. It is the principal gag in the film and a study of its footage will reward any student of editing. The conventional risibilities occur. The wife and the two boys, seated on her

bed, begin to giggle, then start laughing, finally end
guffawing. The camera takes a position on a level with the
footboard of the bed and remains there for a great deal of
the sequence, offering occasional front shots of the trio as
they fall back howling on the bed. The reason for this
low-angled shot is not apparent until the pay-off moment in
the sequence. As the roisterers become progressively drunker
and more hilarious, their laughter and back-slappings force
them back flat on the bed. Now Stan, then Ollie, next the
wife. (It is, incidentally, a great tribute to the essential
decency of the Laurel and Hardy films that a scene showing
two men and a woman all in pajamas laughing and bouncing
drunkenly on the same bed does not have even a faint touch
of suggestiveness about it.)

As the hilarity continues, the camera cuts to the front
door. The woman's real husband has arrived home. The
drunk came to the wrong house. Hubby is, naturally, the
judge who hates drunks and vagrants, and as the camera
follows him slowly, we are suspensefully aware that he is
shortly going to meet several in his own bedroom. Cut back
to the low level bed position, and we see another sequence of
Ollie and his companions slowly dropping down, one by one,
out of sight behind the bedboard. Then follows a superb
"freeze" shot of perhaps five seconds showing the judge
glaring. This is a long time in any film for a static shot but it
arrests us effectively and builds up suspense. The glance is so
cold and baleful that it is almost frightening. Cut back to the
low level shot. The three on the bed are now upright and
jouncing about at the height of their pyramiding laugh build-
up, near to hysteria. Unable to support his merriment, Ollie
drops out of sight, then the wife drops out of sight, then Stan
looks briefly and happily at the camera and drops out of
sight. A three-second hold shot of the bedboard alone, and
then Stan suddenly pops back into view, staring at the
camera with frigid horror. Payoff. Cut back to the judge and
the same merciless stare. Back to the low level and Ollie's
beautifully measured double take as he rises to look at the
camera. The ending of the film is conventional—a tie-twiddle
and a chase in darkness before the fadeout, but the previous
sequence is one of the most brilliant ever done in the comedy
film.

It was this kind of improvisation (much of it worked out
on the set) which resulted in Laurel and Hardy's only Academy Award film, *The Music Box* (1932). It is unquestionably

the finest of their short films,* and it is all the more remarkable because it came at a period of frustration when it seemed their well of inventiveness had run dry. Again, typically, the plot is bare.

The observation has been made that the gag men in the silent days would take inspiration from almost anything they encountered in their daily life. In 1927, one of the Roach idea men was driving through the Hollywood Hills section of Los Angeles. He noticed a very high terraced rise of steps leading from the main street to a house high up on one of the hills. This served as the location for *Hats Off* (1927), the impelling action of which derives from the desire of the boys to get a washing machine to the top. In 1932, at a barren point in the gag men's lives, the suggestion was made that a remake of *Hats Off* might not be out of the way, with one interesting variation—substitute a piano for the washing machine. Increasing the size of anything does not necessarily make for improvement as Cinemascope has so frequently demonstrated, but in this instance the piano was an inspired choice. A piano is a solid and sometimes stubborn thing, and yet it seems to have a life of its own. Particularly in its upright form, it has an almost impertinent stolidity which is at odds with its function. This is the spirit of *The Music Box*—piano against man—*two* men, two earnest, sweating, brainless men who pit their all against The Machine Age which has always and shall always baffle them.

The Laurel and Hardy Cartage Company is delivering a piano. On arriving at the terraced slope, the piano is eased down on Ollie's back, their wagon horse steps forward, and the piano crashes down on him to the tune of an assertive little jingle. The first defeat sets the film's tone. It is a minor defeat; there shall be many more, all increasing in complexity and gravity. As they move up to the first landing, they huff, puff, and grunt; this is hard work. The first landing is a period of rest for them and for us. They reach the second landing a mite more easily. From above, a baby carriage descends the narrow stairs. Impasse. The boys try to shove the piano to one side but it ignores them and slides bumpily down the steps all the way to the street. The maid pushing

---

*Some *aficionados* might argue for *Two Tars* (1932), a great work, in which the boys as sailors are caught in a highway traffic jam and cause the reciprocal destruction device to spread down a long line of cars. Replete with ripped fenders and smashed-in tonneaus, it is hilarious stuff but I have evaluated its prototypes thoroughly at the beginning of the chapter.

the carriage goes past them, laughing, and Stan kicks her in the fundament gently but with emphasis. She slaps Stan and this amuses Ollie. She hits Ollie with the baby's bottle and leaves in anger to inform the cop on the beat. Up the incline again. The camera has now gone to the very top of the hill, and a beautifully composed shot shows the two pushing up in twists and veerings as the faint and slightly discordant tingle-tingle of the piano counterpoints their erratic progress. They reach a position very near the top when, as they stand panting in near-triumph, the cop appears below and yells, "Come down here, you!" Stan shrugs and walks all the way down only to be told that the cop really wants Ollie. Stan shouts up to Ollie. Ollie starts down, after which the Demon Machine comes to life and begins to follow him down with increasing speed. As it bumps down the steps, it gives an increasingly discordant series of sounds which reach their crescendo as Ollie stumbles on the bottom-most step, and the piano glides over him into the street. This damned piano is *alive;* it just doesn't want to get up there.

After a dispute with the cop, up the hill again. Halfway up, the boys meet a top-hatted German professor type (Billy Gilbert) who indignantly demands that they make way for him. Stan knocks his hat off, and the boys watch with great amusement as it sails happily down the steps as the piano did, out into the street to be crushed by a truck. Enraged, Gilbert shakes his fist at them and storms off.

Stan and Ollie reach the top at the psychological moment when we are not able to endure another disappointment. Just as the boys are congratulating themselves and the front doorbell of the house is pushed, the piano tremors slightly and actually makes a turn on the path to go clatter-ding-ding-clatter-bump down the entire terrace—with Ollie hanging on to it, sweeping the ground. It goes out into the street, just missed by the whizzing trucks. We are spared further anxieties by a title, *"That Afternoon . . ."* The boys are back on top in front of the door. The mailman comes up to them and says, "Hey, what's the matter with you fellows? You didn't have to haul that thing all the way up those steps. There's a side road here. You could have driven up!" Stan and Ollie look at each other with sadness at the thought of their abysmal ignorance. What to do now? There is only one thing to do. Grunt-heave-ho! They take the piano down the steps again in order to drive it up the side road.

This is a superb film. Its citation by the Motion Picture Academy of Arts and Sciences as the best short subject of

1932, and Stan Laurel's personal endorsement of it as the best picture they ever made, are the only accolades it needs. It was shot in just a few days and, most interestingly, in sequence. All of the short subjects they did were made in this fashion. A most unusual procedure, the shooting of scenes in sequent order gives to the films a reality and truth to be found in few other comedy films.

In reviewing the advances made by the Laurel and Hardy films from the time they began to use sound, a pattern of homogeneity is evident. By constant experiment, the films had evolved into something singular and definite. The dumb rubes of the first films had now become two personalities. They were invincibly ignorant, always in trouble, but indomitable. They were polite. They were gentlemen. Following the traditional definition of a gentleman, they never knowingly inflicted pain on anyone and yet the world was always inflicting pain on them. How to face up to this? Nothing to do but go on to the next adventure which frequently began with Ollie's pontifical, "How do you do? I'm Mr. Hardy. Mr. Oliver Norvell Hardy. And this is my friend, Mr. Laurel." This unvarying introduction marked them truly. It said in implication, "No matter who you are, wherever you are in life, we are as good as you. We have dignity and we expect dignity in return. We may not get it but it is our right, and we look forward to it and that happy future that perhaps *you*, sir, might lead us to!"

From the technical aspect, the films were unified by a number of factors. Their fundamental idea must be simple, based in reality, and capable of bearing a number of im- provisatory variations. The fact that they were shot in se- quence gave them a natural progression of incident and emotion. Very importantly, Stan Laurel had a strong hand in supervising the films. His editing gave them a rhythm and pace that was geared to pure, free-flowing, functional come- dy. Films like *The Music Box* were the masterpieces of the short form. Artistically, Laurel and Hardy were at their peak.

Chapter VII

THE FEATURE FILMS, THE TOURS, AND FAME

When Jean Cocteau was advised that Cinemascope was now available for his films, he said in solemn tones, "Ah, I shall now have to write on bigger sheets of paper." A parallel point can be made here. Whether or not Laurel and Hardy should have entered the field of the feature film is a matter probably not worth extended debate. There is no question that the films contained some of their best work; it is also undeniable that they carried a high percentage of dross. Stan Laurel, for one, has very little doubt on the matter.

"We should have stayed in the short-film category," he asserts. "There is just so much comedy we can do along a certain line and then it gets to be unfunny. You've got to settle for a simple basic story in our case and then work out all the comedy that's there—and then let it alone. But you can't take a whole, long series of things we do and stick them all together in eight reels, and expect to get a well-balanced picture out of it. We didn't want to go into feature films in the first place, and even though I've got some favorites among them, I'm sorry we ever did go beyond the two- and three-reelers."

In 1931, the year of the first Laurel and Hardy full-length picture, *Pardon Us*, the short feature comedy was still in robust health. The Our Gang Comedies, Mickey McGuire, Charley Chase, W. C. Fields, and others were flourishing but the merry notes of Walt Disney's Silly Symphonies were being heard in more and more theaters. The public taste in comedy seemed to be changing. Cartoons, long the exclusive domain of children, were being geared for the older children. Crudities (Mickey Mouse using the nipples of a baying hound as organ keys) gave way to comparative subtleties (the anvil-

121

clang sound effect created by Laurel and Hardy to accompany a blow on the head). Hollywood was quick to sense the growing importance of the adult market in the cartoon film, and the budgeting for what had heretofore been a sop to the baby trade grew apace.

In 1931, Laurel and Hardy had little thought of cartoon competition. They were fully content doing successful two-reelers. Their initial film in the feature bracket, *Pardon Us,* began as a two-reeler. Hal Roach was distributing his pictures through Metro-Goldwyn-Mayer at the time and as a part of a reciprocal contract, he was given access to various M-G-M facilities. The studio had recently finished *The Big House,* an immensely popular prison picture with the late Wallace Beery. Roach planned to use the M-G-M set for a simple prison-break two-reeler but M-G-M suddenly added a proviso: Laurel and Hardy would have to do a picture for them in exchange. Roach would not agree so he built his own prison set, a very expensive item for a two-reeler. So expensive was it indeed that he added four more reels to bring it into the feature category and, it was hoped, the bigger market.

The result, while generally amusing, is described accurately in Stan's words as " . . . a three-story building on a one-story base." Stan and Ollie make some home brew and sell their first batch to a prohibition agent. The ensuing prison routines are the best thing in the film, sliding off into wild excursions of verbal humor which, enriched by the personalities of the two protagonists, are masterpieces of their kind. One delightful sequence is a classroom scene that might have come straight from a two-a-day vaudeville. It featured the ineluctable Finlayson as the prison teacher. The musical theme for the Roach "Our Gang" comedies establishes the atmosphere of the scene which begins with Fin's entrance in full academic regalia, mortar board and all, into a schoolroom full of thugs and plugguglies. After his customary one-eye squint, Fin catechizes his charges.

> *Fin: Now, then. What is a blizzard?*
> *Stan: A blizzard is the outside of a buzzard.*
>   Fin double-takes powerfully.
> *Fin: Three goes into nine how many times?*
> *Stan: Three times—*
> *Fin: Correct!*
> *Stan: —and two left over.*
>   Ollie laughs immoderately.

Fin: What are you laughing at?
Ollie: There's only one left over!
        Fin doubles his previous take.
Fin: All right, now. Spell needle.
Ollie: N-e-i-d-l-e!
Fin: There's no 'i' in needle.
        Stan leaps to his feet indignantly.
Stan: Then it's a rotten needle!

Finlayson's reaction to this almost knocks him out of camera range.

The boys' customary uncomprehending conflict with authority ultimately sends them to The Hole, a dank, unlighted room where they are to languish for a month. A great moment of lunacy is reached when Stan stops the guard just before he is to enter his long stretch of oblivion. "Pardon me," he asks, "do you have the time?" Ollie's camera look is piteous and lingering.

Up to this point, the film has been of a piece. Now the patchwork begins to show. For no reason other than that there are extra reels to go, the boys escape to the cotton fields down South. Here bromidic sequences of colored cotton-pickers singing low are introduced along with one equally unrelated yet very entertaining scene featuring the musical talents of the two leading actors. They have disguised themselves in blackface. Captivated by the singing of the field hands, they swing into a chorus of "Lazy Moon," Ollie singing it in a good tenor and Stan doing an eccentric slide dance of quiet and graceful inanity. They return to the fields as pickers but are captured when a dog licks off Ollie's coloring while he is repairing the warden's car, fortuitously stalled near the fields. Back they go to prison and accidentally forestall a prison break which insures them pardons.

The ending of the film has a significant moment in respect to the analyzing of their characters. The warden, played by Wilfred Lucas, an English actor capable of giving the adjective "august" full significance, is presenting them with their pardons and some beneficent advice. "Boys," he says, "—and you *are* my boys!" The boys warm up cozily. They are children in need not only of a loving but of an *understanding* father, willing to explain the world and its strange ways to them. "Boys," he goes on, "those warning shots you fired in the dining hall saved us from a disaster of *cataclysmic* proportions!" This is becoming difficult to follow. They frown in slight apprehension. Perhaps this father-figure—like the rest

of the world—is not going to be able to tell them where to
look for that happy future. "Boys," the orotund tones roll on,
"I want you to look on these few months of your life here as
simply a *hiatus!*" Stan's eyelids, glued together it seems with
kindergarten paste, open slowly and stare in massive bewilderment; Ollie's eyes jerk open wider in profound vacuity.
Once again the world has failed them. In a previous scene the
warden calls them "babes in the woods," probably the best
succinct description of Laurel and Hardy ever uttered.*

Their second feature film, *Pack Up Your Troubles*
(1932), suffered from the serious defect of *Pardon Us*:
desultoriness. A World War I comedy, it details the boys'
search for the grandparents of a little girl whose father has
been killed in France. The address of the grandparents is
unknown, but the boys have a clue. The people are named
Smith. Their project of finding "Mr. and Mrs. Smith" with
only the New York telephone book as their guide provides
some good, although intermittent moments of fun. Stan has
been gone all day on a mysterious search of his own, and
when Ollie peevishly demands to know where he has been,
Stan tells him that his journey has been unavailing. "I went
all the way to Poughkeepsie and this ain't them," he says
sadly. "Poughkeepsie?" Ollie asks. Stan nods sorrowfully and
holds up a Smith Brothers cough-drop box. Ollie fumes in
exasperation.

The finest episode in the picture is brief. It is also touching
and wildly funny. As originally conceived, Ollie was to take
the little girl in his lap and tell her a fairy tale to soothe her
to sleep. The gag is built on reverse procedure. Overcome
with fatigue, he begins to tell the story but the child interjects
and aids him in the telling of it. She prattles on happily with
the rest of the story, lulling the story-teller into slumber. At
the time of shooting the scene, Babe Hardy pointed out that
Stan's character fitted the gag better than his. The substitu-
tion was made, and the result is humorous and affecting. This
typical unselfish gesture of Babe's points up the meaning of
the word "team."

At the completion of *Pack Up Your Troubles*, Stan and
Babe were ready for an extended rest. They had vacationed

---

*Pardon Us was filmed in four other languages, French, Spanish,
Italian, and German, using four separate casts. Laurel and Hardy, both
monolingual, wrote their lines on a blackboard out of camera range
in their own phonetic approximations of the sounds spoken to them
by a language coach. *Pardon Us* was the only feature done in this
fashion. Five two-reelers were similarly produced before the practice
was abandoned.

now and then through the years but they had never gone much beyond the confines of Hollywood. Stan's hobby as well as his profession was the creation of humor, and the Roach lot was a home away from home. Babe concentrated on his golf game when not before the camera. This was their life and a good one, but by 1932 they needed change. They had been turning out their comedies for almost seven years. Babe wanted to go to Canada, and Stan decided to take his family to England to see his relatives in the North Country. He planned to rent a car, drive through all the old scenes of his boyhood, perhaps fish a bit, and rest, rest. Babe was caught up in the project when he heard that the golf clubs in Scotland were probably the finest in the world. They would go together. Their train trip cross-country was uneventful. Then Chicago. Without warning, while changing trains for New York, they were caught in a surging mass of fans, photographers, and reporters. They were stunned. Kept close to the home lot, not much given to the granting of interviews, they actually did not know how famous they were. In New York the crowds were gigantic. Newsreel cars followed them riding down Broadway. The crowd became so great that policemen pushed the two thoroughly astonished comedians into Minsky's Music Hall to escape suffocation.

They sailed on the *Aquitania,* but life here was not easy either. They were followed everywhere, dogged by autograph hounds, and assorted gawkers. The docks at Southampton were swarming with masses of people who had waited hours to see them. As Stan and Babe appeared on the gangplank, the crowd whistled the Laurel and Hardy theme song in unison,* cheered, clapped, roared. The crowds were so great that they forced an hour's delay of the train for London. The arrival at Waterloo Station was full pandemonium. In the desperate struggle to get through to his car, grimy and exhausted, Stan was almost swallowed up. Babe *was* swallowed up. He found himself pulled and tugged and petted, caught in the midst of hundreds of fans. He fled only after great exertion and pleading. An afternoon press reception had been arranged for them at their hotel, the Savoy, and they arrived at it without even a chance to wash.

They saw Noel Coward's *Calvacade* the next evening at

---

*This theme, "The Cuckoo Song," was used as the opening music for a morning program emanating from a radio station housed on the Roach lot. Attracted by its breezy ridiculousness, Laurel and Hardy recorded it for one of their early pictures. A preview audience laughed at it and it became their permanent theme.

Drury Lane and took bows standing in the royal box. Later
in the week, on their way to a personal appearance at the
Empire Theatre which had been hastily arranged for them,
mobs rushed the car at Leicester Square and tore off a door.
At the theater they were greeted with a prolonged frenzy of
applause that they could not believe. A tour had been arranged by M-G-M to cash in on this approbation and everywhere the team went—Birmingham, Manchester, Edinburgh—
the reception was repeated. When they arrived in Newcastle,
Stan, as a near-home town boy, was feted with a thoroughness that left him unnerved. In Glasgow, thirty people were
hospitalized because of the crush. When they went to the
continent to escape the press of attention, the President of
France sent his car for them and they rode like conquerors
down the Champs Elysées to their suites provided for them
without charge by Claridge's. Worn out, they returned briefly
to England, thence to California. Their vacation was over,
such as it was. Not one fish had been caught, not one round
of golf played. They were totally unprepared for the attention shown them. For the first time in their lives, they
realized that they were more than ordinary working comedians. They were in the household-word category, and the
wonderment of that was never to cease.

In returning to work, although the general pattern of
future progress had not been envisioned, the remaining significant work of Laurel and Hardy was to be devoted to the
feature film. Of the eighteen films they were to do for Roach
before leaving him in 1938, twelve would be features and the
remainder two- and three-reelers.

The mixture as before in their feature releases, good
comedy mixed with banal, frequently extraneous straight
plot, continued. Much of the imperfect nature of these films
was to come in the assignment of various talents to create
the films. Laurel and Hardy did not now have as much to say
about the actual making of some of these films. This is
evident in one of the first pictures they made after returning
from abroad, *Fra Diavolo* (1933),* a lighthearted version of
Auber's opera. *Fra Diavolo*, despite its faults, has moments
of great comedy, and is one of Stan's favorite films. On the
credit side, it is a period picture. The world of the past was
an ideal milieu for them, the boys believed; and this film,
with its eighteenth-century atmosphere, its lords, ladies, and

---

*Released in most areas as *The Devil's Brother*. The working title
and the title always used by Stan Laurel in referring to the film is
Fra Diavolo.

robber captains, was where two nitwit servants belonged, the servants who traditionally provide the comic relief in romantic comedy.

In the instance of *Fra Diavolo*, the relief was not enough Pare Lorentz in a perceptive review for *Vanity Fair* puts the charge:

> What should have been the most interesting picture of the year has turned out to be an uneven slapstick comedy with musical sequences which, unfortunately, are so poorly done they seem unrelated to the antics of Laurel and Hardy [who] make up for the long stretches of narrative stupidity with their first rate music hall pantomime.

The film's defects are the result of a two-director dichotomy. Hal Roach himself directed all the "plot" footage and musical numbers; Charley Rogers did only the Laurel and Hardy sequences. Three of the routines from these sequences are music hall masterpieces, almost independent of the need for sound. The first is a drunk scene which is as good as most things out of Chaplin. This scene (also to be done later in an interesting variation in *The Bohemian Girl*) shows the boys drawing wine in the cellar of the inn where they are staying with their master, the Marquis de San Marco, alias "The Devil's Brother" (Dennis King), an infamous bandit of the region. At his hest, they are drawing a few flagons of an old vintage which is to be drugged and given to the stupid and rich Lord Rocburg (Finlayson).

Ollie stands on a ladder leaning against the huge cask and draws the wine from a spout above. He passes a full flagon to Stan, takes an empty one from him and goes back to the spout as Stan pours the full flagon in a large pitcher. The pitcher is duly filled and Stan is desperate for another source of deposit. It does not occur to him to tell Ollie that the wine is ready. He has been directed to hand over and receive the flagons and that is what he will do. Obviously there is nothing for it but to pour the wine down his throat, and he accordingly bottoms-up a number of them as the sound track plays a drunken, wavering rendition of Auber's Fra Diavolo theme. The great comedy in the scene lies in the ever-increasing unsteadiness of the drinker, a gag which in unsure hands would be tedious. The subtle build-up of besottedness, the gradually increasing eye-bulging and weaving of torso, the steady growth of the volume of lip-smacking are admirable touches, and they are all of a piece. There is an intercut sequence of Fra Diavolo wooing Lady Rocburg (Thelma Todd) which serves as an indication of the passage of time but it is not necessary here. Such is the cumulative effect of the Laurel pantomime that at its conclusion one can almost see wine oozing out of every orifice.

The other two pantomime scenes enlivening the film have for their point of origin ideas so simple as to seem childlike. The word is deliberate because not only are the best Laurel and Hardy routines easily understandable to children, in the two instances here they actually derive from childhood games. Stan, like many English children, engaged in imaginative and mysterious little set-games as well as in the more robust activities of rugger and cricket. One of these can best be described as the "finger-wiggle" in which both hands are clasped palms down, fingers interlocked, with one center digit sticking out above and the other center digit below. The game, such as it is, is to accomplish this with dispatch and then wiggle the central fingers frantically but rhythmically. The other game, of a more complicated nature but requiring equal dexterity, is called in the film, "kneesie-earsie-noseie." The player slaps both knees, then pulls his nose with his left hand while he simultaneously pulls his left ear with his right hand. He again slaps his knees and reverses the pulls. It is not an easy thing to do slowly; it is practically impossible to do it, as Stan does, in quick time.

In both games in the film, Stan does them casually and with easy grace. Ollie is irritated initially, then puzzled, finally intrigued. He sets about to try them and, inevitably, winds up in a burst of anger at his inability to bring them off. There are parallel follow-ups with the attempts of the landlord (Henry Armetta) to do the same. Audiences seeing the film have been impelled psychologically to join the game, and in 1933 it was not an uncommon sight to see film-goers leaving the theater with hands on nose and ear or wiggling fingers in frantic agitation.

This is the realm of nonesuch in which Stan Laurel gloried. It is intrinsic to the fabric of the lively, colorful entertainments of the pantomime in which he began his theatrical career in England. One of the next Laurel and Hardy features, *Babes in Toyland* (1934), is basically a pantomime. Stanley Dum and Oliver Dee, apprentices to the Toy Maker, are boarders with Mother Peep. Santa Claus places an order with the Toy Maker for six hundred soldiers, one foot high. Stan, in characteristic confusion, makes one hundred soldiers six feet high, to universal horror, but when the Bogey Men attack Toytown and send the inhabitants scurrying off in fright, it is Stan's toy soldiers who save the community. *Babes in Toyland,* a nine-reeler adapted from Victor Herbert's operetta of the same name, had two directors like its predecessor among the feature films, but here much more harmony obtains. Gus Meins directed the many children and Charley Rogers again supervised Laurel and Hardy. It is the best Laurel and Hardy film for children alone.

As the financial success of the feature films grew, Hal Roach determined to keep his stars in that field. The artistic success of the films was a sometime thing, and it gradually became apparent that the full-length form was too extended for the solid but comparatively tiny Laurel and Hardy bag of tricks. *Bonnie Scotland* (1935) has all the typical vices and virtues of their feature films. *Variety* condemned the structure of the film as being weak, specifying that the two subsidiary plots, the love story and the semiserious Bengal Lancers adventure story, are mostly independent of Laurel and Hardy and evoke little attention. The indictment is true. And *Variety* also unwittingly summed up the reason why Laurel and Hardy flourished both in silent and sound films, in English and non-English speaking countries, with the comment: "As usual, the boys talk as little as possible."

By 1936, Laurel and Hardy had been a team for ten years. Those years were transitional ones for film comedy. There was the obvious change wrought by sound but another significant alteration impended. Physical humor was becoming outré. The musical comedy star from Broadway typified at its best by Al Jolson and Eddie Cantor became fashionable. The spate of film musical comedies from the mid-thirties on through the war years of the forties was a prodigious one. Their music for the most part was unremarkable and the comedy too many times was the sort epitomized by a pouting Allen Jenkins chewing on a toothpick and moaning, "Gosh, boss, if you put that skinny lil dame from the chorus inta the lead, then we got trouble, heap big trouble, get me?" William Boehnel in the New York *World-Telegram* cried out for the old days:

The opportunities to see low comedy on the screen are becoming less and less frequent each season now, as old masters of slapstick are either disappearing from the screen altogether or are modifying their erstwhile tactics to such an extent as to be unrecognizable. Such being the case, you who still retain memories of Charlie Chaplin, Buster Keaton, Harry Langdon, and the others would better drop in at the Rialto this week and see *Our Relations* which seems to have all the earmarks of old-time low comedies.

Our Relations (1936) shows Laurel and Hardy with a firmer grasp on the feature-length form. This was at least partially due to the fact that Stan Laurel himself produced the film. Roach continued to act as executive producer but the details of production fortunately were left in Stan's hands, and the result shows more concentration on the purely comedic aspects than heretofore. *Our Relations,* although taken from W. W. Jacob's famous story "The Money Box," has a closer affinity to Plautus and Shakespeare. It is *The Comedy of Errors* in mufti. Stan and Ollie have two seafaring twins, Alf and Bert, who come to town and engage in mistaken identity misadventures until they are reunited in the final footage.

The critical and financial reception to *Fra Diavolo* three years before had lingered with Hal Roach, and in 1936 he took another old opera, Balfe's *The Bohemian Girl* and warmed it up for his (by now) leading comedy stars. As in *Fra Diavolo,* there were two directors but they were both essentially comedy men. Jimmy Horne and Charley Rogers knew the characteristics of the Senseless Ones and the result is that comedy lives everywhere in *The Bohemian Girl.* The music does not impede the comedy since it is limited to two songs, and both of them fit into the plot as pleasant musical interludes. The New York *Times* felt that "Mr. Balfe probably wouldn't approve of what Laurel and Hardy have done to his *Bohemian Girl.* Then, again, being Irish, perhaps he would." The plot, with its princess-stolen-by-gypsies, serves as an innocuous framework for a series of pantomime routines.

In the search for original feature vehicles (the rejuvenated opera format seemed to be played out), the Roach gag men entered into a Golden Age of ideas for the extended form. In *Way Out West* (1937), they created the only Laurel and Hardy Western, notable for the singing and dancing done by the stars. In *Swiss Miss* (1938), the idea men dreamed up a Swiss-folk-schmaltz festival which initially posed the nice problem of how to get the boys to Switzerland with some faint degree of probability. The obvious answer was to cast them as mousetrap salesmen who must needs go to the country producing the most cheese. *Swiss Miss*'s high point of hilarity has been called by James Agee one of the genuinely great moments in film comedy. And it is, despite some curious studio interference that in the final edited version leaves part of the sequence meaningless. As the scene stands in its present form, the boys are lugging a piano across a swaying rope bridge a thousand feet over a Swiss gorge. They are halfway across when they meet a gorilla coming from the other side. The involvements of the gorilla, an exasperated Ollie and a tipsy Stan make a chillingly funny episode. Despite this, an integral part of the gag is missing. As originally conceived, the piano contained a bomb triggered to go off when a certain key was struck. It was planned that the many twistings and turnings of the three, especially the accidental falls of the intoxicated Stan against the keys, would add much more strength to an already suspenseful scene. For some incredible reason during the cutting process, the bomb idea was deleted (Stan was not consulted), and the film in its present form contains meaningless shots of Stan crashing against the keys. And yet, despite this partial disemboweling, the scene fully justifies Agee's evaluation. The day after seeing *Swiss Miss,* Bosley Crowther of the New York *Times* said he was " ... a recent Laurel and Hardy convert—as recent as yesterday."

His conversion might have come earlier if it had not been for the curious revisions by the studio in some of the major films of feature length, originally edited by Stan Laurel. The *Swiss Miss* alteration is the most serious example of this. One of the directors has suggested a reason.

"In directing quite a few of the pictures," comments Charley Rogers, "I became aware of a curious paradox about Hal Roach. He knew Laurel and Hardy were his biggest money-makers. I know he liked the boys personally and they always got along very well with him, but there was something odd occasionally in his feelings about the pictures. He wanted the pictures to be successful, of course, but sometimes it almost seemed that he would unconsciously do little things which harmed them. Or maybe he just didn't understand. Maybe it was because he had a first-rate comic mind but never had the chance to learn the business of putting comedy on celluloid himself. It always puzzled me.

"But one thing is certain. He had the imagination to picture the boys as a team, and he had the vision to let them, by and large, create their own comedy in their own way. Please remember I use the word 'unconsciously.' Maybe Hal got too busy being a businessman but of course he sure as hell had to be that. I think maybe he got too much in the habit of saying 'Know what I mean?' when he was trying to explain a comedy idea of his and just leaving it up to somebody else to figure out what he meant and do it for him. I'll never know, but I do know that he was always a good man to work for."

Swiss Miss and only three other films, *Blockheads* (1938), *A Chump at Oxford* (1940), and *Saps at Sea* (1940) are almost completely worthwhile in the feature field. Thereafter, there is retrogression. It is, perhaps, not pertinent to speculate on what might have happened if they had returned to short subjects. For one thing, the shorts were out of fashion. And worse was to come: a change in studios and the resulting loss of supervision of their own work brought the poorest Laurel and Hardy films before the public at a time when they needed hits to win followers among the newer generation. But in the early years of the forties, they were in green pastures.

Blockheads would be memorable if only for a scene that Chaplin might envy: Stan standing guard in a trench twenty years after the Armistice. He has never been relieved by the corporal of the guard, and as he pivots an about-face (his pacing has hollowed out another trench), the camera pans slowly past him to show a mountain of the empty tin cans of beans he has consumed in twenty years.

Saps at Sea and *A Chump at Oxford* were both originally conceived as four-reelers, a compromise between the short and feature length, but were given added footage to enter the full-length market. The increase shows padding but at base these are both good films. *Saps*, like its predecessors, hits its best moments when pantomime holds sway. Typical is a scene in which the boys are forced to digest a meal of twine, lamp wick belt, caked talcum, and liquid tobacco which the villain (for whom the meal had been prepared) forces them to eat. The boys had prepared these items, respectively, as spaghetti, bacon, biscuits, and coffee in the hope of incapacitating their captor. Their variations on the swallowing process and their attempts to be amiable through waves of nausea are charmingly graphic. In *A Chump at Oxford,* Stan undergoes a brief and complete metamorphosis of personality absolutely unique in all the Laurel and Hardy films. It is discovered that Stan is actually Lord Paddington, formerly Oxford's leading undergraduate, who left at the apex of his career, a victim of amnesia. An accidental blow restores him to his former status as the greatest athlete and brainiest student ever to enter the school. He cows a crowd of bullies and throws them, one by one, into a ditch, and ultimately achieves a pinnacle of splendor by acquiring Ollie as a manservant. Ollie's camera looks as the lordly Stan addresses him condescendingly as "Fatty, old thing" are heartrending.

At this high point in their artistic fortunes, it may be well to pause and ponder an early question, is there a Laurel and Hardy *form?* If so, what is its essence? A hint may be found in this inspired doggerel:

SIR ANDREW:	Sir Toby Belch! How now, Sir Toby Belch!
SIR TOBY:	Sweet Sir Andrew!
SIR ANDREW:	Bless you, fair shrew.
MARIA:	And you too, sir.
SIR TOBY:	Accost, Sir Andrew, accost.
SIR ANDREW:	What's that?
SIR TOBY:	My niece's chambermaid.
SIR ANDREW:	Good Mistress Accost, I desire better acquaintance.
MARIA:	My name is Mary, sir.
SIR ANDREW:	Good Mistress Mary Accost—
SIR TOBY:	You mistake, knight . . .

Twelfth Night, I, iii.

William Shakespeare wrote these words in 1601 for the two leading comedians of his company to whom an old tradition attributes the physical qualities of fatness and leanness. Here Sir Toby Belch, the fat and fatheaded, and Sir Andrew Augecheek, the lean and lean-witted, employ a verbal gag of the kind Laurel and Hardy would use if Christopher Fry instead of H. M. "Beanie" Walker had written their dialogue. Laurel and Hardy come from a great tradition of clowns—from the rogue servants of Greek comedy, the buffoons of the *commedia dell' arte,* the Bottoms and Dogberrys of the Elizabethan theater, the red-nosed comedians of vaudeville and the music halls—and it is a compound of all of these that constitutes their comic quotient.

Are they really funny? The universal popularity of their films would seem to make this question rhetorical, but there are enough dissenters in the neighborhood of the arts, at least, to suggest that the question should be put. In an attempt to assess the popularity of Laurel and Hardy among professionals in their own business a number of comedians and writers of comedy were asked, among other things, if they thought Laurel and Hardy were funny and if so, why. Over ninety per cent of those approached unhesitatingly plunked for the affirmative, and of those who cried nay, it is interesting to note that they said without exception that although they did not really enjoy the films they felt it was possibly because of a lack in themselves. "I'm *sure,*" said a prominent English writer of film comedy who did not want to be identified, "that they are funny although for the life of me I can't tell why. I once saw Charlie Chaplin during a showing of one of their films curled up with laughter. That shocked me. To me, Laurel and Hardy are simple comedians, pleasant and childlike, and, I should think, capable mainly of entertaining children. I see few subtle things in their work. They are banana-peel-slide comedians for all I can see. But I daresay I'm wrong. I shouldn't care to call anything unfunny that Chaplin enjoyed."

Heading the list of the yea-sayers is Steve Allen who defines their basic aspect as funny men: "I have always heard that the critics looked down on Laurel and Hardy, and that only 'the people' approved of them. In this case, time would seem to have shown that the critics were wrong, although we must not suppose that it always will. The people are just as apt to err as the critics, but probably no more so. As a child I found Laurel and Hardy always amusing. My opinion has never changed. As to why they were funny ... first of all, Laurel and Hardy *looked* funny. Certain comedians have this tremendous beginning advantage, in that audiences are amused before a word is spoken. Personally I have always had to work just a little bit harder to overcome the fact that I don't *look* like a comedian. And when I *do*—as for example when I work as 'The Question Man'—I find it very easy to get laughs. So Laurel and Hardy were funny to look at—the dopey guy and the fat man, and both of them in ill-fitting, somewhat Chaplinesque clothes."

This, also, to Groucho Marx is the beginning point of their humor. He says, "You ask me if I find them funny. I don't find them at all these days but when I do, I find them funny. And I find them funny, among other reasons, because Stan Laurel had a skinny neck and Oliver Hardy a fat stomach. As to why they are *really* funny, I leave that to the professors and the savants. I gave up trying to find out why people are funny a long, long time ago."

The matter of their appearance is cardinal to their appeal, in the opinion of Frank Nugent who reviewed them in the New York *Times*, May 4, 1937: "Too many books are being written on the anatomy of humor and none on the humor of anatomy. If ever we get around to it, we intend to do a special chapter on Messrs. Laurel and Hardy who scampered into the Rialto yesterday in an irrepressible little slapstick called *Way Out West*. In it we should mention that they would not be funny if both were fat or both skinny; or if the cherubic Mr. Hardy could not arrange his dimples into a perfect pattern of pained resignation; or if the long-jawed Mr. Laurel was not, by the very cut of his jib, the model of a complete dolt. Nature meant them to be anatomically funny men, and there's nothing much one can do about nature, not even a script writer."

This is universal comedy and made of perdurable stuff. Jack Benny, who calls them "two very funny gentlemen" remarks on an additional quality, encompassing all that is fundamental in humor. "Their humor will always be great," he insists, "because they do not rely on jokes. Instead, by placing themselves into basic situations and then having something go wrong, they are understood by people of all ages and all walks of life. And just like Charlie Chaplin, their comedy is appreciated all over the world by people who do not speak their language or know the customs or habits of the United States. Physical and expressive humor has been popular since the early days of comedy and this explains the popularity of clowns from the early days to today. Jokes may become outdated, but the type of comedy Laurel and Hardy did will always live with us."

This is echoed by Steve Allen who reaffirms Benny's statement that their humor appeals to all classes. "You must remember," he points out, "that those of us who deal in humorous ideas can only appeal to audiences intelligent enough to understand our ideas. Laurel and Hardy, however, can make the egghead and the modern Neanderthal both laugh by sticking to physical humor and simple situations. Of course they could also include some very clever and inventive gags such as that in which Stan's and Ollie's wives fire a shotgun blast while chasing them around an apartment building. At the sound of the shot about twenty-five guys jump out of various windows, some of they carrying their trousers.

This may be a little blunt, but one has to admit it's very funny. Oddly enough we showed a film clip of this particular gag on my TV show and received not a single postcard of complaint, at a time when there were perhaps twenty-five million people watching. No—the type of comedy they did never goes out of style. The public has lost interest in other comedians, especially since television has speeded up the natural evolution of comedy, but Chaplin and Laurel and Hardy will always be funny in any part of the world."

Clearly then, Laurel and Hardy, (a) look funny, and (b) have a primary focus on the physical gag. But there is something more that gives them distinction and causes them to be loved by millions. Points (a) and (b) can also apply to the Three Stooges. The extra dimension of Laurel and Hardy is suggested by Eddie Cantor who has fond memories of their work. He defines his admiration: "It is their seriousness that strikes me most forcibly. They play everything as if it might be *Macbeth* or *Hamlet*. That, to me, has always been a true sign of comic genius. In addition, they have two very important things going for them. One is the utter frustration of Hardy, and the other is the 'one-beat-behind-every-other-person's-thinking' of Stan. He was always late, and always wrong, and underneath that frightened face, we always get the idea that he loved Ollie."

The relationship between Stan and Ollie which Eddie Cantor has pointed up is, in Allen's words "partly of the traditional sort: that of the stupid character and his somewhat smarter friend. But Ollie was no ordinary straight man. He was funny himself in his wonderful ability to portray exasperation at Stan's stupidity and the predicaments into which it thrust the two of them. There are probably resemblances and influences between Laurel and Hardy and 'Norton' and 'Kramden', as portrayed by Art Carney and Jackie Gleason in their great Honeymooners' sketches. Carney was the dope and his dumbness would eventually drive Kramden into wonderfully funny rages, sometimes manifested in an almost irresistible urge to hit Norton."

The logic motivating Laurel and Hardy's world is, of course, splendidly illogical. Henry Morgan speaks of their "way of looking at the sequence of events in what would otherwise be an orderly process. Usually, when a man does A, the next logical thing to happen is B. Laurel and Hardy proceeded on the assumption that it was just as logical for A to be followed by C and the audiences laughed because they recognized that though C *was* an additional possibility, they had just never thought of it that way. At the same time, the audience assumed that C would never happen to a person of intelligence—the old 'superiority' explanation of what makes people laugh."

What of Laurel and Hardy in terms of the one thing that links them closely to Chaplin, the art of mime? That they are superb pantomimists may not be abundantly clear at the first jog of memory. Yet running through their films is a kind of mime which, although not as deliberately conceived or as consciously artistic as Chaplin's, is, nevertheless, valid and beautiful in its comic context. Marcel Marceau, one of the greatest mimes in the world, has two idols: Chaplin and Stan Laurel. There are two reasons for this idolatry. In 1950, M. Marceau was an unknown, laboring in a far from fruitful vineyard. Pantomime, as an active art, had long been absent from the theater, and Marceau was determined to bring it back to its days of glory in France when it had been exalted by Deburau, the great mime, and his peers. During a personal appearance of Laurel and Hardy in Paris, Marceau asked Stan to visit a tiny, suburban theater to see the young Marceau company and its repertoire. After seeing the beautifully touching program, Stan arranged for a press conference and introduced Marceau to the reporters as an unsung genius. He praised the little company fulsomely and within a very short time, Marcel Marceau attained his rightful recognition as one of France's great artists.

It is not only because he is Laurel's protégé, however, that Marceau is devoted to him. "All mimes in the world today owe much to Stan Laurel," he points out. "To them, Stan Laurel is a *maître*. He is of the mime that goes back through history to the very oldest days of the juggler and the comic troubadour. In those days they did not need much of a story. What they had principally was *lazzi*—or comic tricks. These perhaps look simple to people—like bumping into someone you don't see at first and then backing off in surprise and fear—but these things are not easy to do and do gracefully and do *funnily*. It takes much practice to do this in a very funny way. Now, there are many people who can do these things in a funny way but it is only a master like Stan or Charlie who can do these things in a very, very funny way to make us laugh out loud, heartily. Stan comes from the same school as Charlie—the music hall. And so many great artists come from there. They all speak the universal language of the movement of the body. They can be both comic and tragic, sometimes at the same moment. Both Stan and Charlie have different styles, of course, and Charlie developed more into social comedy, but they are basically the same kind of comedians if you watch them closely.

"Like all comedians, they know that laughter is a question of society. Everything relates itself to society—the things we do—the things we do in relation to other people. Whatever we look at we look at in terms of others—even of animals. All things we laugh at remind us of other people or other things. All things in comedy are a reaction to other things. Hardy always reacts to Laurel when he does something wrong. Hardy is like the crowd which always surrounds Chaplin. Chaplin, for instance, always fights with policemen and Hardy always fights (a little fight) with Stan. And there is such fun when you see the two of them matched in a fight—the tiny, thin Stan against the big Hardy who could smash him down in a second but never does. That is why we laugh at them and love them. They are so opposite. You see, that's why Chaplin always used big men opposite him, like in *The Gold Rush*. Chaplin is the *real* law—the little man, the average man—against the big man, the brute force of authority—the *unreal* law. David and Goliath—and this is a law of the theater—the law of contrast. Laurel and Hardy knew this law and they lived it and acted it beautifully on the screen. And they had comedy of character as well in addition to this comedy of contrast. They are very endearing men. They are very noble men because there is no evil or thought of evil in them. I can see this in them personally, too. Stan Laurel is personally a good man, and most charming, and simple in the best sense of that word. And I am told that Babe Hardy was the same kind of man. Now, all these things I have told you are things that great comedians need but they also need something else and that is *control*. That is why they are great in mime, because they know how to get a very simple effect by a very simple movement of the body. It is simple but it takes much time and effort to learn how to *be* that simple. That is why they have lasted so long in addition to the other reasons I have explained."

Laurel and Hardy lasted twenty-nine years (1926-55) as an active working team, and yet in all that time their basic gags were not many and they remained the same. Clearly, then, there is a deep, basic quality—dare one call it spiritual?—that kept them in public affection for so long, a quality transcending the mere oddity of physical appearance, pantomimic ability, and gag cleverness. This element permeated their work and it is inherently their brightest glory. The quality is *innocence*.

Basil Wright, the gifted British documentary filmmaker, sees their inherent purity as a battle of fate. "Fate always finds them unprepared, though Hardy, in silent anguish, mimes his certainty that it is only to be expected that it is, as usual, Laurel's fault. Which Laurel cheerfully admits, but wonders still at the Providence which turns each innocent gesture into the willful smiting down of his friend and partner." Why does Stan do this? David Robinson, writing in *Sight and Sound*, answers that Stan is not " ... perhaps so much a fool as a child. (In *Be Big*, his preparations for a day in Atlantic City consist of packing his toy yacht.) This child's innocence is a quality which Hardy shares with him, and which is, perhaps, the leading distinction of their comedy work. They are the most innocent of all the clowns ... The motives which impel them have a childish logic; their jealousies and meannesses (they have been known to deceive each other) are mere babyishness. When Stan drinks (it is usually Stan who drinks) it is about as vicious as a cigarette in the bathroom. In their films they are often given wives; but to them a wife is no more nor less than a kind of starchy, unyielding, unsympathetic governess, to be deceived (in simple things), outwitted and escaped for the afternoon. Stan and Ollie are, of course, always recaptured. Extramarital interests are on the erotic level of taking an apple for the lady teacher."

And this, if anything can be, is their form—innocence and blessed ignorance, out of tune with the sins and follies of the world. *This* is their artistic essence: no comedians in history were ever so innocent so funnily, so endearingly. "Where ignorance is bliss, 'tis folly to be wise," goes the old saw. This is exactly the state of existence of Laurel and Hardy. Their innocent ignorance makes them the epitome of all the Babes in all the Woods. The world is against them, and they care—but they do not mind. They are too eternally young to hold grudges, so they face the world with hope renewed daily, hourly. Their optimism is indestructible. Their ignorance is truly invincible because it is the angelic armor of perpetual childhood.

After all the experts have spoken, after all the reasons for their longevity have been catalogued, the final decision is rendered, as it has been always, by the public. Henry Morgan puts it: "They were expert clowns; and if ever you're in doubt as to whether they were funny or not and why, remember: they made people laugh!"

Chapter VIII

"HE REALLY IS A FUNNY, FUNNY FELLOW"

In 1940 it seemed to Laurel and Hardy that the opportunities to make people laugh were becoming fewer and fewer. They did not then know it but their days of greatness in the films were over. There had been rumors and rumors of rumors in the film industry that Stan and Babe had quarreled. Jealousy was whispered as one of the reasons for dissension and some substance seemed to support the gossip when Babe made a Roach film, *Zenobia*, without Stan. Rumor could not have been much farther out. Both Laurel and Hardy had been under individual contracts with Roach, each terminating at a different time, all during their years as a team. It was the feeling of both Stan and Babe that some attempt should be made for them to exist legally as a team which was not possible under their contractual agreements with Roach. Stan's contract terminated in 1939 and he decided to wait until Babe would be free of his the year following. In working out his contract alone, Babe did *Zenobia*, an undistinguished comedy about Southern life, and it did not advance his reputation. The appearance of Harry Langdon in the film may have been accidental or may have been, as some thought, an attempt by Roach to create a new Laurel and Hardy without Laurel. This was foredoomed. Hardy without Laurel was H_2 without the O. In 1940, free of their Roach contracts, they formed Laurel and Hardy Feature Productions. The organization was never to make a film.

At the termination of their long association with Roach, new possibilities beckoned. A yearning to appear again before live audiences was strongly appealing, and they planned a revival of Victor Herbert's *The Red Mill* with dialogue revised for their screen characterizations. During the process

141

of rewriting, they did a one-night stand for the Red Cross at the San Francisco World's Fair in a quickly written skit presenting them as applicants for drivers' licenses. Next they toured in *The Laurel and Hardy Revue,* a full-length show with sixty-five people including variety acts, a line of girls, and a closing thirty-minute Laurel and Hardy sketch. *The Red Mill* plans were put aside permanently when the *Revue* toured to good business for three months in the Midwest and East. After a USO tour in the Caribbean area with a stream-lined version of their *Revue* act, they returned to the States playing Chicago and Detroit before Babe's laryngitis forced them to close prior to a Boston date.

They had been away from films for almost two years in 1941 when they entered into association with two film com-panies, Metro-Goldwyn-Mayer and 20th Century-Fox. They made the agreements assuming the most basic assumption possible—that they would make them in the characters of Stan Laurel and Ollie Hardy, the two lovable, singularly eccentric cotton-wits who had entertained the world and his brother for many years. It was an assumption sturdily ig-nored by both studios. To evaluate the results as charitably as possible, these films should not have been made.

There is, in all these films, a surface resemblance to the Laurel and Hardy of old but that, alas, is all. Gone is the old charm of the grown-up babes in the woods. Everywhere is the attempt to fit them into situations not native to them. They were now forced to do what long years of work in creating the two characters told them they should not do.

On the set of their first film for 20th Century-Fox, *Great Guns,* a war picture, they were given their marching orders. It was: do it the studio way or not at all. Any attempt to do things the old way, the Laurel and Hardy way, was not only resisted but put down. *Great Guns* shows this division of interests clearly. It is almost as if they are doing their stuff under water. The sharp edges of their characters are rounded by cliché comedy. Their familiar trademarks are almost completely erased, and what is more unforgivable, their beautifully intelligent unintelligence is gone. They exist simply as stupid boobies.

The second film for 20th Century, a mystery "comedy," *A-Haunting We Will Go* (1942), featured Dante the magi-cian who is shown in a sequence with the boys and a coffin. The coffin contains a body and the depressing byplay around it, evidently intended for humorous purposes, comes over as precisely antithetical to comedy.

Jitterbugs (1943) was worse. It now seemed certain to Stan and Babe that the studio was attempting a deliberate freeze-out. They had protested against this cavalier treatment, and it became obvious that the studio in order to discountenance further opposition was allowing the artistic level of the films to sink lower and lower without actually allowing them to be brought out as absolute garbage. It seemed as if the studio was throwing them into any kind of story and giving them elemental production facilities, hoping at the same time that the Laurel and Hardy names would bring in a certain amount of business. Whatever the reasons, these pictures show a descending scale of ineptitude in conception and production. From bad to worse to the worst.

Jitterbugs has a scenario that does not make sense. *The Dancing Masters* (1943) was not quite as good as *Jitterbugs*. *The Big Noise* (1944) failed to live up to the standard set by *The Dancing Masters*. The plot and comedy of *The Big Noise* can be put into a sentence: the boys had to deliver a powerful bomb. They did. *The Bull Fighters* (1945), a thing of patches and shreds, using scrap background clips taken from the recently completed 20th Century film, *Blood and Sand*, lacked the strength of *The Big Noise*.

The two films for M-G-M, *Air Raid Wardens* (1943) and *Nothing But Trouble* (1944) were the mixture as before without, perhaps, as much seediness in production as in the 20th Century offerings. *Air Raid Wardens* had an added handicap in the presence of a Civil Defense official who resented any kidding of air raid procedures. The possibility that humor can be a superb teaching instrument never occurred to this gentleman, whose insistence on deletions eliminated the only passable fun in the picture. *Nothing But Trouble*, based on the old film plot of the boy-king, was typical of the last banal work of Laurel and Hardy. These films constitute a swan song of deafening discords.

"What was there for us to do but get out?" Stan asks with bitterness. "We had no say in those films, and it sure looked it. We had done too many films in our own way for us to keep taking anything like that, so we gave up the ghost. It was sickening."

They waited. Great comedy stars with a long heritage of unique films do not always find an easy outlet for their abilities when cut suddenly adrift. After a period of enforced rest, they were approached by an old friend, the English impresario Bernard Delfont, who asked them to make a tour of the music halls of the British Isles. They accepted with pleasure, not a little of which was contained in the anticipation that perhaps this tour would allow Babe to get in his golfing and permit Stan to see his cousins, two hopes left unfulfilled because of the public clamor during their first visit. Life became zestful again. Stan's private life, occasionally upset by divorce-court litigation, had a happy-ever-after culmination in his marriage to Ida Kitaeva, a Russian singer. The boys revived the old driver's license sketch, and in 1947 they sailed for England.

If they expected a diminution of public attention, they were not to receive it. In all of the leading cities, the crowds came full surge, frequently causing extension of playing dates. But Babe had a chance to play golf and Stan saw his cousins. Best of all, he visited his father, A.J., for many good talks. Living with Stan's sister who operated a pub in Grantham, Lincolnshire, the old man glowed with pride when Stan walked in, the toast of the North Country and indeed of all England.

Their stay in the United Kingdom was cut off at the end of nine months because Babe's alien status would not allow further work. Without any qualms about language barriers because of the act's pantomime, they toured Sweden, Denmark, Belgium, and France before record crowds. In France a tactical error: they presented their work in a night club. The necessity to stay near the microphone and the lack of opportunity to improvise sudden bits of pantomime (which was *de rigeur* when they were shooting pictures) prevented success in a "room." But this was the only failure. The first of three working tours abroad, each would be made under unvarying conditions of public acclaim.

It was a source of quiet pride for Stan to think back, during the tours, of the old days in 1910 when he and Charlie Chaplin had left British shores with little more than pocket money as their possessions. They had both done rather well for music hall comedians. Charlie had never been in much doubt as to the splendor of his future; Stan was sure of nothing but his growing ability to make people laugh. Their paths had not crossed much in the years between the silent days and their current eminence. A brief hello in a restaurant or a casual wave of the hand across the street was the limit of their social meetings. During the 1947 tour, Stan became friendly with Hannen Swaffer, the acerbic old Fleet Street journalist. Swaffer gave Stan a copy of his latest book which he had inscribed to Chaplin. "He asked me to give it to Charlie," Stan recalls, "and I said I would. When I returned to California, I thought at first I'd mail it to him but after thinking it over, I changed my mind. We had barely seen each other all the years in the States. There we were, such old friends, but somehow our paths just never seemed to cross. So I finally made an appointment with him at his home in Beverly Hills. I intended just to give him the book and chat a few minutes. When I arrived, he was delighted to see me and gave me a grand welcome. The few minutes stretched on into seven hours. We sat and talked and talked about the old days, what had happened to So-and-so in the troupe, and all of that. He really came out of his shell and was the old Charlie I knew when. I've never seen him since. Wrote him a couple of times; no answer. But that was a wonderful day."

Despite Laurel and Hardy's success in the halls and variety theaters on their tours abroad, their hearts always remained in motion pictures. It was considerably heartening, therefore, when they received an invitation from a producer in France to do a film. Conditions could hardly have been better. France is a country devoted to Laurel and Hardy. The French cinema traditionally gives full working rein to its artists. Moreover, the film was to be done quickly—in twelve weeks.

It took twelve months.

Atoll K (1950)—released in America as *Utopia*—was the last film Laurel and Hardy made. There is not much to be gained in dilating its melancholy history. Stan says simply: "It was an abortion. Part of the cast was talking French, some were talking Italian and there were the two of us, the stars, talking English. Nobody—and that includes the director and us—knew what the hell was going on." The film bears out his statement. Based on the idea that a tax-free Utopia is possible on a desert island, *Atoll K* plods from tired gag to pointless situation unendingly. During the making of the film, Stan became ill, had an operation and dropped from 165 to 114 pounds. Barely able to stand up during some of the shooting, only his sense of obligation forced him to see it through. He contracted diabetes, and the team returned to America, dispirited, their future obscured.

In the months that followed, Stan slowly regained his health and in 1952 he was strong enough to undertake another nine-month tour of Britain in a railroad-station sketch based on an early short film, *Night Owls*. In 1953, they returned for a third extended tour, and again they played to capacity houses in a hospital sketch featuring them as professional whiskey tasters. On their way over for this, their last professional engagement, an incident occurred that demonstrated as probably never before their place in the hearts of the people who had been seeing their films for so many years.

They were docked at Cobh, Ireland, and word had reached the city that Laurel and Hardy were on board. The docks were swarming with many hundreds of people. "It's strange, a strange thing," Stan says in recalling that day. "Our popularity has lasted so long. Our last good pictures were made in the thirties, and you'd think people would forget, but they don't. The love and affection we found that day at Cobh was simply unbelievable. There were hundreds of boats blowing whistles, and mobs and mobs of people screaming on the docks. We just couldn't understand what it was all about. And then something happened that I can never forget. All the church bells in Cobh started to ring out our theme song, and Babe looked at me, and we cried. Maybe people loved us and our pictures because we put so much love in them. I don't know. I'll never forget that day. Never."

They returned to the States in 1954 and, for all they knew, permanent retirement. But in 1955, Hal Roach, Jr., who had taken over his father's studio, became aware of a phenomenon. Many of the old Laurel and Hardy films had been sold to television distributors, and stations in many American cities were featuring local Laurel and Hardy weekly programs. Fan mail reached astounding proportions. Thousands of telephone calls plagued television studios. Where *were* Laurel and Hardy, these questioners demanded. Were they still alive, still making films? Laurel and Hardy Feature Productions was, in fact, legally alive but at rest because producing capital was not available. Although not in personal financial difficulties, Stan and Babe were not wealthy men. They did not receive a penny from the television showings. This, in itself, was not galling since they had worked for good salaries in the Roach days, but they were angered at the knowledge that their names were being used to advertise deodorants, hair oil, beer, and floor wax without their remuneration or consent. They contemplated a suit to keep their names free from such usage but a previous legal battle by Roy Rogers along similar lines had failed. They could do nothing.

Young Hal Roach wanted to give them a chance to reach their old greatness. The time was ripe. Laurel and Hardy fan mail was on the increase. They had been toasted on Ralph

Edwards' *This Is Your Life* program. Happily, an agreement was reached with Roach that they were to make four hour-long television features, and it was especially comforting to realize that they were going to be the old Laurel and Hardy, doing what they knew best, working under their own artistic conditions. The films were to be done in the spirit of the English music hall pantomimes Stan had always loved. The atmosphere was to be that of the never-never land of the fairy story and the children's book. The Babes in the Woods were literally to come to life. Laurel and Hardy were back and on their own terms. Ten days before shooting was to start, Stan had a stroke.

As strokes go, it was not a critical one. "Not so deep as a well" but enough to postpone production plans for a considerable period. Able to walk but hampered by a pronounced limp, Stan turned all his energies to recovery. Progress was gradual and then, suddenly, Babe became ill. Under treatment for some time because of a heart condition, he was told to lose weight. At the time of the last English tour he had weighed well over 300 pounds, and now within weeks, he dieted down to 185 pounds. He seemed to be making progress when he, too, was felled by a stroke, a heavy, degenerating one that left him incapable of movement and speech. Babe Hardy had never been sick in his life. In the year after his return from the final tour he suffered two heart attacks which he kept quiet because he did not want people to know. Shortly before his stroke he had suffered a gall bladder attack but surgery was prevented by his heart condition. In the winter months of 1956 as he waited impatiently for his health to be restored, the thought that his popularity was on the upswing again made his illness all the more unendurable. Mrs. Hardy says, "His spirits seemed to improve when we brought him home from the hospital, but he got frustrated by his inability to do things. He would sit and look at a newspaper and then get irritated because he couldn't absorb it. We put him in a wheel chair one day and brought him into the den to see TV. He was always such an avid watcher. But it was evident that he couldn't comprehend what was going on. Sometimes he got so upset over his inability to get better that it seemed he almost wished it was all over with." Night and day nurses were required for the long months. The doctors told Mrs. Hardy that there was no hope for recovery but she continued in a brave and valiant fight helping to nurse her husband through his illness which was terminated fatally August 7, 1957.

"I was terribly shocked when Babe died," Stan said. "I had just got through answering hundreds and hundreds of letters of good wishes from old fans all over the world who were praying for him, lighting candles for him. He was like a brother to me. We seemed to sense each other. Funny, we never really got to know each other personally until we took the tours together. When we made pictures, it was all business even though it was fun. Between pictures we hardly saw each other. His life outside the studio was sports—and my life was practically all work, even after work was over. I loved editing and cutting the pictures, something he wasn't interested in. But whatever I did was tops with him. There was never any argument between us, ever. I hope wherever he is now that he realizes how much people loved him."

Today Stan Laurel lives in a modern apartment-hotel in Santa Monica by the ocean which he loves so much. It is a stimulating experience to watch him as he looks at TV, particularly when he watches his old films. This writer noted that at these odd times he seemed to be watching Babe most of the time, and asked why. "I don't know why I watch Babe all the time," he said. "I guess it's because the character fascinates me so much. He really is a funny, funny fellow, isn't he?"

Suddenly a commercial crashed heavily on to the screen and a look of genuine pain crossed his features. "Look at that! That's why I hardly watch our pictures anymore. It upsets me so damned much to see how they turn the plot of our pictures into a hash. We worked so carefully to get the sequence of action just right in the editing process, and then some idiotic fool comes along and cuts the film up in big chunks just to squeeze in a mess of advertising. Continuity, establishing shots—most of them gone. The pictures just don't make sense on television. I'd rather they'd show them entire or not at all. That's why I don't look at us much. Why see a lot of good hard work turned into a jigsaw puzzle? I'd even be willing to edit them for nothing but I know they don't care."

And what of modern film-making? Would he get back into it if he could in any way? The answer is strongly negative. "Absolutely not. The trouble with modern picture-making is the lack of time for preparation. I guess they have to rush because the cost of everything is so fantastically high these days. In the old days we made good pictures, had fun doing it, and didn't get apoplexy every five minutes because something was running overtime. If we didn't like things in previews, we'd do them over again—maybe more than once. I couldn't do pictures the way they do them now. Hollywood is a rat race today."

He sat still for a moment and looked thoughtful. "Well," he said, "how about a good fish dinner at that restaurant down the highway?"

The thought occurred, following Stan and his wife down the stairs and into the car, that it might be interesting to ask him if, after all these years, he still thinks comedy. Did the ideas—so many of them absolutely unique—keep coming to him even though the days of active creation were long past and buried? But the question might be tactless so it was forgotten. But not for long.

It was answered, unbidden, as Stan sat pensively in the restaurant waiting for his entrée. He had been unusually silent for a long moment, thinking intensely, and now the thought rushed out. The icy-blue eyes twinkled. He looked at his wife and his guest.

"Just thought of something," he said. "There's a big hotel, see—with thousands and thousands of rooms. The management asks Babe and me—we're plumbers—if we can install the plumbing overnight. 'That's impossible!' I tell them. Babe turns to me and he says, 'What do you mean, *impossible?* Stanley, there is no such woid in the English language as *impossible.* Remember—that if you put your mind to do a thing, you can do it. *Nothing* in the world is impossible. Just tell me. Tell me. Tell me *one* thing that is *impossible!*"

Stan mimed Ollie's ponderous loftiness as he gave the speech. He continued, "Well, I look at Babe for a moment after that. I scratch my head and then I say, 'O.K.! I know something that's impossible—*striking a match on a cake of soap!!*" He leaned forward to his audience and immediately assumed Ollie's camera look of sad and long-suffering disbelief.

The sudden gust of full-blown laughter from the table startled fellow diners in the room but Stan did not notice them. He was looking out over the ocean and he was smiling.

THE REST
OF THE STORY

When this book (consisting of the previous chapters solely) was published in 1961, the Laurel and Hardy revival was in highest swing. The television showings across the country had increased from their already high rerun frequency, various movie producers were planning full length programs featuring excerpts from the Roach films, and (perhaps ominously) the film cognoscenti, the cultists, were beginning to adopt Laurel and Hardy. Their recognition as artists was complete.

It is now that I must forsake an author's anonymity and take a personal role in telling what happened after 1961 to the present. But to tell the full story, which in its essence is the detailing of the endearing qualities that made up the man Stan Laurel and which his genuine modesty would not permit me to say in this book as first printed, I go back to our first meeting when the book was certainly the farthest thing from my mind.

In 1953 I was in England, a doctoral candidate at The Shakespeare Institute of the University of Birmingham, living at Stratford-on-Avon. I travelled to Birmingham once a week for research in the University library, and on one of these trips while walking down a side street I was taken aback at the sight of a billing: "Laurel and Hardy in BIRDS OF A FEATHER—Now Playing—The Hippodrome." Funny. As a Laurel and Hardy buff, I fancied that I knew all their films by title at least, but this was new to me. I went to the Hippodrome and found to my surging delight that the boys were there in person, appearing in a sketch which, as I was to discover, Stan had written and staged.

As I took my seat, and during the variety acts preceding "Birds of a Feather," the thought which occupied me primarily was a nagging fear that perhaps the boys might not be as funny in person as they were in films. After all, removed from a working condition which allowed them to correct error or experiment until the gag flowed easily, might they not be forced into a conventional, trite, comic situation on the stage? Was the principal attraction now to be simply the fact of their personal appearance? In effect, would they be funny? They were funny.

As "Birds of a Feather" rolled along it became quite clear that Stan and Ollie were truly children of the music hall. Although they could not do pratfalls or knockabout turns (Stan at the time was 63, Babe, 61—both looking at least ten years younger than they were), and although they could not perform magic tricks which only the camera would countenance and sustain, they were truly the film characters the world knew and loved, set now in the warm, natural habitat of vaudeville.

The orchestra swung into the tuh-tum-tee-tum beat of "The Dance of the Cuckoos" to introduce the act, and the roar of recognition from the audience was in itself an exciting experience. The curtains parted to reveal a street scene. Ollie entered, looked at his watch impatiently, and walked off. Stan came on, looking properly nebulous, and failing to find Ollie, went out. Ollie came back on, same business, and this was repeated with Stan until finally they passed each other, nodded, said "how do you do," and did big mutual double-takes at the sides of the stage. It was the first big laugh of a continuing crescendo of them. This is not the place to treat of "Birds of a Feather" in full, but its tone is implicit in its central situation: the discovery by Laurel and Hardy that there is employment open to them in a distillery as whiskey tasters.* The second scene occurs in a mental institution where Ollie is a patient. It seems that after tasting whiskey all morning, he was so pleased with his job that he had a couple of doubles to celebrate. By then he was so happy that he decided to leap out of the window and fly around with the birds. When Ollie demanded indignantly of Stan "Why didn't you stop me?" Stan said, "Well, I'd been celebrating too, and I thought you *could* fly." The rest of the sketch consisted of hilarious misadventures with an eccentric doctor and a silly nurse.

At their curtain call, Stan and Ollie came to the footlights, Stan first, Ollie standing behind him in exasperated hauteur. Stan began to speak, Ollie tapped him imperiously on the shoulder and motioned him aside. Stan deferred to him with

---

* Laurel and Hardy buffs need not fear that "Birds of a Feather" is lost to them. I will reprint it in full in a forthcoming book on Stan Laurel.

eye-blinking vagueness and his hands thrown up in his "Well, I didn't know, did I?" gesture. At that instant, in stepping to the microphone, Ollie became Babe, and Stan relaxed into his own person. It was the first indication I had that his off-screen self was the exact opposite of his screen self. His eyes bespoke high intelligence and awareness.

"Thank you so much, ladies and gentlemen," Babe said, "for accepting our little bit of nonsense in the spirit in which it was intended. We especially want to say hello to our friend . . .", and here he mentioned a name which meant nothing to me, "who is celebrating his seventh birthday today!" There was applause as Babe and Stan blew kisses to a beaming youngster in a box, surrounded by family and friends. (I learned later that Laurel and Hardy did this almost every performance to honor a birthday boy or girl in the cities on their tour.) Babe went on: "Stan and I have had a lot of fun appearing before you. Thank you, goodbye—and God *bless!*" Loud, warm applause, and it was over.

As I left the theatre sharing the cozy, almost familial spirit of that audience, I was not only bemused by thoughts of the typical Laurel and Hardy buffoonery I had just seen, but by the appearance of the two men at curtain call as well. For just a tantalizingly few seconds, I had been permitted to see them outside the cocoon of their screen personalities, and I was much intrigued. What were they *really* like, I wondered, as I attained the street and walked slowly toward the railway station. Curiosity aroused and grateful for the splendid entertainment, I wondered whether I should go backstage and thank them personally. I did something then I have never done, before or since: I flipped a coin to force a decision. Blest be that coin.

Any apprehension about my reception vanished when I met them, and the truly heart-warming thing about this was the knowledge that the cordiality and friendliness were genuine. They had no reason to impress a total stranger of little status with a display of kindness. The kindness was there, instinctive, pure-bred, pervasive. It was obvious after a few minute's conversation with both men that manners—plain, old-fashioned manners—were stamped indelibly into their functions as human beings. The courtliness of Hardy and the graciousness of Laurel were bed-rock real, and for a reason that I still quite cannot fathom, I found this startling. In retrospect, I suppose that it was because I realized that the innocent gentility that marks their screen characters was also deeply resident in them as men. It was rather like discovering that Santa Claus really existed.

But there were really no other resemblances to their screen selves, I soon found out. Indeed, in a very real sense, they were almost the opposite of their screen personalities. Oliver Hardy was actually a rather shy person, not given to extravagant gesture or statement; Stan Laurel was ebullient, quick-witted, sharp. I had promised myself not to extend my visit beyond the conventional drop-in so my moments with Oliver and Lucille Hardy were few, but rather a different situation presented itself with Stan Laurel. His wife was away visiting a girlhood friend in Paris, and I sensed that he was somewhat lonely. I was happy to take advantage of the fact.

As Stan answered my questions (which immediately centered on the way the films were created) I watched him closely. Of medium height, his face and figure no longer retained the slimness of his film days, but he was not overweight. (As a diabetic, he had to watch his diet carefully.) His red hair and blue eyes made me wish that Laurel and Hardy had made more than one (obscure) Technicolor film.* As we talked, I became aware that his natural speech was North Country England: strong first syllable emphasis, a measured, even pace—almost a drawl—which he used deliberately for comedic emphasis. Like any great comedian, he was keenly aware of climax, and his sentence endings and carefully planned afterthoughts were used as comic punctuation—the punch-word, the punch-phrase. He had the pleasant habit of uttering something extremely grave which contained a kernel of complete nonsense. Then when his listener became aware of the absurdity and began to laugh, Stan counterpointed the laugh with his own—a high pitched, full-bodied laugh, funny in itself—a laugh of stylish dimension, a laugh perhaps best characterized as a refined horse laugh. There is nothing disrespectful in this description. That tremendously joyful and vital laughter is my happiest and most poignant memory of him. A laugh like that should never die. It contained the laughter of all the world; it was sharp, perceptive, utterly joyous.

He laughed a great deal. And when he did, anyone within sound of that laugh was carried along with it, and went a very far journey.

When, inevitably, we came to the subject of why people

Tree in a Test Tube, made for the Government during World War II.

laugh, he became characteristically modest, disclaiming any real knowledge of why people laugh, but he was quite willing to talk about the things that caused laughter.

"I've got something here," he said, reaching into his wallet to pull out two tattered newspaper clippings. "Listen to this." He read: "London Daily Mail. April 6. *He Stopped Five Million Pound Blast And Gets Five Shillings.* An explosion which could have wrecked the centre of a five million pound steelworks and killed many workmen was avoided yesterday— for five shillings. Steelmen were waiting to charge one of the giant furnaces at a plant alongside Cardiff docks with scrap metal for melting. A hundred yards away a crane driver was moving the scrap from a stockpile of old war material. He spotted an odd-looking object dangling from his magnetic grab and lowered it twenty-five feet for a second look. The odd-looking object? A two-hundred and fifty pound depth charge. The crane driver was given a reward of five shillings."

As Stan finished reading the clipping with great gravity, he folded it and his face slowly drew up into a grimace primed with laughter. "The poor bastard!" he said, and then roared with laughter. "Five million pounds saved—and they gave him five shillings. I'd like to have been there when they did that. And sometimes people tell me that our pictures are unreal!" He unfolded the other clipping. "Somebody sent this to me the other day. It's from the London *Evening Standard*. The heading of the story is 'Groom Chewed Gum at the Wedding—Until the Vicar Stopped Him'. Listen to this. 'It was a church wedding, and it was going according to plan until suddenly the minister paused. He halted the service. And he refused to carry on—*until the groom stopped chewing gum.* Now the minister, the Reverend Frederic K. Chare, vicar of St. Philip's Church, Camberwell, has called for an end to 'displays of bad manners' at weddings in his church. He said: 'The pity is that most of the people guilty of these things have not fully realized that what they have done is wrong. In the normal course of events they rarely if ever attend church. They are more at home in a cinema.' Congregations sometimes hummed and whistled jukebox melodies while waiting in church for weddings to begin, said the vicar."

Stan brimmed over again with laughter and said, "If that isn't a Laurel and Hardy situation, I never saw one. Can't you just picture Finlayson as the minister, me as the bridegroom and Babe as the best man—maybe with squeaky shoes? That's where I get some of the best ideas for the pictures—from life, from some silly but really human situation. Of course in music hall, here with 'Birds of a Feather,' you have to be broader, and you get more unreal. But for our films I don't have to dream very hard to find the crazy things that are real. Oh, wait. I just remember. I've got another one. This would make a beautiful Laurel and Hardy two reeler."

Again he reached into his wallet for a clipping and read it with sober emphasis. "Onion Eaters To Compete. World Title. London Daily Mail Exclusive. Wilfred Pickles is to be asked to judge the world raw onion eating championships to be held at Ashington, Northumberland, on January 26. The championships are being staged because of the success of the All-Britain Contests held in Newcastle two months. The winner was 26-year-old Walter Pinchen, a Newcastle lorry driver, who ate a twelve ounce onion in two minutes, fifteen seconds. A few seconds behind him was the Northumberland and Durham champion, Mr. Joe Fitzpatrick, a 38-year-old miner. Mr. Pinchen and Mr. Fitzpatrick are favorites for the world championship."

Stan's laughter cascaded. "Yeah, they'd be world champions almost—until they came up against Laurel and Hardy when they put their brains to it!"

We talked of this and many other things until I realized with a start that the next show was virtually upon us. I apologized for overstaying my leave, and he replied gently that it was a pleasure for him to talk comedy, and please to feel free to come back whenever I liked. A literal soul, I took him up on this, and our future conversations unwittingly took the pattern of question-and-answer as if in documentation for an article or book on the comedic devices of Laurel and Hardy. That idea came to me in one of the sessions when I asked him if anyone had ever approached the two of them with a proposal for a book. He admitted that from time to time authors had suggested a dual biography but that he saw scant merit in these ideas because he thought there was little to write about. "What is there to my life but just making a lot of comedy?" he asked. What indeed.

When I suggested to him that a worthwhile book might be dedicated to just that endeavor—a study of him just making a lot of comedy, he thought it might be worth doing if enough people existed who wanted to read about such things. I told him a potential publisher would worry about that, and so work on the book began.

In the months that followed, when I saw him on tour in the English provinces and later at his home in Santa Monica and his apartment in Malibu, it became very clear to me that his statement about the flux and bend of his existence was literally true: comedy *was* his life. It was not an obsessive thing; it was the natural thing. It was the milieu in which he worked and lived and thought and relaxed—the fish in his water. And basic to all of this was his instinctive gentleness— a quality he shared with Babe Hardy, and undoubtedly one of the conditionings which allowed them to work so surely and fully with each other.

As Stan told me in the first letter he sent shortly after the idea for the book was germinated, Babe Hardy was not especially concerned with fleshing out the research on the comedy-making material. Always polite and helpful to the extent of his general interest, he left the matter of the comedy analysis to Stan. It was, after all, he said, Stan's business. This, as I discovered, was another reason why the team of Laurel and Hardy functioned so well. As incredible as it may seem, Babe Hardy thought of himself primarily as a straight man—the sounding board for the comedian of the team. It is understatement to say that Oliver Hardy is the funniest straight man of history—past and to come.

As I worked with Stan, I noticed that although his gentle demeanor was imbedded, he was capable of what the Old Testament calls righteous anger. This was rare but when it came it was full-fashioned. He displayed normal irritation over the inequities of existence like segregation which he regarded as sinful, but I only saw him rush into livid anger twice. The first was when I asked him about his days at Twentieth Century-Fox and the second was the moment when he finished reading a story about himself by a reporter for a London paper. His anger was all the more formidable for its contrast with his usual soft-spoken, self-contained manner.

The 20th Century-Fox matter was a grievance of long standing and the memory of it burned and rankled. When at times in my note-taking I would set down instances of rather cavalier treatment of Stan by persons in his earlier working life, he frequently asked me to tone it down because it distressed him to hurt people even if, as it seemed to me, he had ample reason to give a certain gentleman or lady the back of his hand. But when it came to the shabby way in which the executives of 20th Century-Fox treated him by rudely refusing to let Laurel and Hardy be Laurel and Hardy, he was almost savage.

"About those boys," he said, "I don't care how rough you treat them. I can't tell you how much it hurt me to do those pictures, and how ashamed I am of them. We wouldn't have done them if we didn't have to eat. I kept thinking that sooner or later they would let us do the pictures in our own way, but it just got worse, and we couldn't take it anymore. I didn't always see eye to eye with Roach, but for the most part he left us alone, and I'll always be grateful to Hal for that. But those Fox people! You can give it to *them* good."

(I would add as a passing note that if I did not give it to them good at the proper place in a previous chapter, I will do so now briefly by saying that the non-artist who circumscribes or harrasses the artist in his work is, by precise definition, a nothing.)

On the other matter that excited Stan's full anger, it was, I believe, particularly galling that the incident was the work of an Englishman. Stan never paraded his nationality, but he was proud of it and always retained his British passport. In this situation of which I speak he had granted an interview to an English journalist, given him lavish hospitality in the beautifully furnished Laurel apartment overlooking the Pacific, and had expected, at the very least, honest reporting. The journalist left in an effusion of thanks and good fellowship.

A few weeks later Stan was astounded to receive a letter from his sister in England expressing anxious concern over his financial condition. Similar letters arrived from friends abroad. A number of French journalists flew in from Paris with a substantial check representing a collection taken up by the readers of a large French newspaper which had conducted a campaign to help, in their words, "this poor and ailing genius." After asking the Frenchmen (who were astounded at the poshness of his apartment) to turn the money over to charity, Stan quickly tracked down the source of all this misinformation to the English newspaperman. This worthy had written a sob-sister story for his paper in London in which Stan was presented as a forlorn, sick, impecunious man, forgotten by Hollywood and the world.

The story distressed and angered him so much not only because a sensation-hungry fellow countryman was the source but also because it was the germ for a popular impression, still current among some people, that Stan was a poor man. For the record, let it be said here plainly that Stan

Laurel, although no longer a wealthy man, was far from a poor one. To use a phrase which surely everyone understands, he was well off. He left his *widow* well off.

But irritations like these, as painful as they unquestionably were, did not disturb the even and pleasant tempo of his life. After my book was first published in 1961, his fan mail increased considerably, and he took great pleasure in reading this mail and answering all of it despite the fact that this was done at some expense to his health. His wife, Ida, agonized at times to see him severely strain his eyes (which had been gradually weakening) in reading the mail—particularly the hand-written letters, some of which looked as if they had been scrawled in moving box-cars. But she was satisfied that the letters meant a great deal to him although she wished that their volume would diminish.

Another thing which pleased him greatly was the special Oscar that the Academy of Motion Picture Arts and Sciences awarded him for his contribution to film comedy. He loved his Oscar but he made very sure that there was no undue solemnity attached to its ownership: he dubbed the statuette "Mr. Clean."

After this book was published, there was no need for me to see him much in person, and this together with the fact that we were on different coasts, caused our communication to become chiefly one of letters. But I never dropped the old habit of asking him about film comedy, or comedy of all kinds for that matter, and it is a special joy of mine that from my letters and my notes I am able to construct a very thorough picture of his ideas and opinions on comedy. There is no space to do that here but I think it would be of interest for me to present at least a sampling of his opinions. I have divided them into two basic categories, likes and dislikes, but I emphasize that this is a partial listing only. He liked and disliked a large number of other comedians and performers.

LIKES

Oliver Hardy—"So terribly funny. He can still make me laugh like crazy after all these years."

Charlie Chaplin—"Just the greatest."

Harry Langdon—"A great comedian who had it in him to be a great actor, like Chaplin."

Buster Keaton—"Another 'great,' and I use that word very carefully, not the way Milton Berle uses it. One of the reasons why I love Buster so much is because he lives comedy as well as practices it. Some of his things are better than Chaplin's."

Billy Gilbert—"One of the top rank. I wonder why more people didn't know that?"

Eddie Cantor—"He and Jolson were wonderful entertainers the like of which you don't see anymore. They weren't comedians really, but funny singing entertainers of the kind I used to see and love in the English music hall. It's a shame that young performers these days aren't even remotely like them."

Jack Benny—"A real craftsman. He knows what consistent comedy characterization is. The only criticism I have to offer is that once in a while he holds after his laughs too long. He milks those 'holds' on occasion and he shouldn't."

Jack Paar—"Something rare these days—a wit."

Jerry Lewis—"He keeps imitating himself, but he has much talent and I think in time he will do first rate comedy. I hope so. But he's going to have to learn artistic discipline."

Dick Van Dyke—"If ever they do a film of my life—and I hope they won't—I'd like Dick to play me. He's one of the very, very few comedians around who knows how to use his body for real comedy."

James Finlayson—"He could just lift that eyebrow, and I'd break up."

Harold Lloyd—"He hardly ever made me laugh but I admire his inventiveness. A smart comedian. The best of the straight comedians."

DISLIKES

(I know that Stan's kindness would make him insist I keep the next three gentlemen's identities a secret.)

Mr. X—"I can understand why people laugh at him. I do myself once in a while, but rudeness is rudeness. I just don't care for it. I know X overdoes it deliberately, but I still can't enjoy it. The only thing that saves him from being terrible is that he can be witty occasionally."

Mr. Y—"The same thing applies to Y as to X—but Y lacks the occasional wit."

Mr. Z—"Very funny when he's not being dirty. I can't stand him."

Red Skelton's Breaking Up—"Dreadful. Just dreadful. I love his talent but I hate the thing he does with it when he does that deliberate and undeliberate breaking up. In my opinion this is the worst possible thing any comedian can do—the worst. And he even lets some of his untalented guests do it. Dreadful."

95% of Stand-Up Comedians—"They're so alike. The same dark blue suits, the same tired jokes about how skinny or how fat or how stingy their wives are. The best thing I could wish for them is that they had wives like the kind they describe."

Television M.C.'s—"Who are these people? What are they? I don't understand this business of their being billed as 'stars.' What are they stars of? Who made them stars? As far as I can see, they don't do anything but read some questions from cards or a machine. The terrible thing about some of them is that they think they can act or read funny lines well or even ad-lib funny lines, for God's sake. And even worse than that is the fact that the audience seems to accept them on these terms. These people aren't talents, or even bad talents. They are simply *non*-talents."

That last withering blast summed up one of the essential qualities of Stan as a creative man. He loved talent, he deplored bad talent or misuse of talent, and he scorned non-talent masquerading as talent. "It's the old well-known fact," he once said, "you can't make something out of nothing. But, my God, how they're trying."

Not long before he died, I helped found an organization devoted to Laurel and Hardy along the same lines as the Sherlock Holmes group, The Baker Street Irregulars. Our group derives its name from a Laurel and Hardy film in which the boys give their loyalties to a national lodge called "The Sons of the Desert." Stan was delighted with the idea and when I drew up a constitution for the organization he approved it and gave it two delightful emendations. Here it is in its final form:

THE SONS OF THE DESERT
Article I

The Sons of the Desert is an organization with scholarly overtones and heavily social undertones devoted to the loving study of the persons and films of Stan Laurel and Oliver Hardy.

Article II

The founding members are Orson Bean, Al Kilgore, John McCabe, Chuck McCann and John Municino.

Article III

The Sons of the Desert shall have the following officers and board members who will be elected at an annual meeting:

Grand Sheik

Vice-Sheik	*Grand Vizier*
(Sheik in charge of vice)	(Corresponding Secretary)
Sub-Vice-Vizier	*Board Members-at-Large*
(Sheik-Treasurer and in charge of sub-vice)	(This number should not exceed 812.)

Article IV

All officers *and* Board Members-at-Large shall sit at an exalted place at the annual banquet table.

Article V

The officers and Board Members-at-Large shall have absolutely no authority whatever.

Article VI

Despite his absolute lack of authority, the Grand Sheik or his deputy shall act as chairman at all meetings, and will follow the standard parliamentary procedure in conducting same. At the meetings, it is hoped that the innate dignity, sensitivity and good taste of the members assembled will permit activities to be conducted with a lively sense of deportment and good order.

Article VII

Article VI is ridiculous.

Article VIII

The Annual Meeting shall be conducted in the following sequence:

    a. Cocktails
    b. Business meeting and cocktails
    c. Dinner (with cocktails)
    d. After-dinner speeches and cocktails
    e. Cocktails
    f. Coffee and cocktails
    g. Showing of Laurel and Hardy film
    h. After-film critique and cocktails
    i. After-after-film critique and cocktails
    j. Stan has suggested this period. In his words: "All members are requested to park their camels and hire a taxi; then return for 'One for the desert!' "

Article IX

Section "d" above shall consist in part of the following toasts:

    1—"To Stan"   2—"To Babe"   3—"To Fin"
    4—"To Mae Busch and Charley Hall—who are eternally ever-popular."

Article X

Section "h" above shall include the reading of scholarly papers on Laurel and Hardy. Any member going over an 8½ minute time limit shall have his cocktails limited to fourteen.

Article XI

Hopefully, and seriously, The Sons of the Desert, in the strong desire to perpetuate the spirit and genius of Laurel and Hardy will conduct activities ultimately and always devoted to the preservation of their films and the encouragement of their showing everywhere.

Article XII

There shall be member societies in other cities called "Tents," each of which shall derive its name from one of the films.

Article XIII

Stan has suggested that members might wear a fez or blazer patch with an appropriate motto. He says: "I hope that the motto can be blue and grey, showing two derbies with these words superimposed: 'Two Minds Without a Single Thought.' "

These words have been duly set into the delightful escutcheon created for The Sons of the Desert by Al Kilgore. They have been rendered into Latin in the spirit of Stan's dictum that our organization should have, to use his words, "a half-assed dignity" about it.

We shall strive to maintain precisely that kind of dignity at all costs—at all times.

The co-founders and the current membership have nurtured The Sons of the Desert to the point where it now rejoices in Tents in many places. We are deeply proud that the last job of work Stan did was a listing of prospective members he thought we should welcome to our fold.

Stan's last years were richly pleasant. There was one hospital stay because of a diabetic episode, but his spirits were unflaggingly high. He was delighted that Lucille Hardy's loneliness had been ended by a very happy marriage to Ben Price, and he talked frequently on the telephone with old cronies like Ben Shipman, his loyal friend and lawyer dating all the way back to the early Roach days. President Kennedy, whom he admired greatly, sent him an affectionately inscribed photograph—as a fan. Friends, most of them made through correspondence, came to see him weekly and found him unfailingly cordial and warm. Above all, he gloried in the love and the care of his wife, Ida, who watched over him with the precise amount of solicitude he needed. She shared all his full memories with him, and it was she who unwittingly gave him probably his most fitting epitaph.

In telling me once of the details of her life with Stan, she talked of many things and then concluded quietly with what almost seemed to be an after-thought.

"And oh!" she said, "how we *laughed!*"

Laurel and Hardy Film Listing

These listings are inadequate and some of the dates are only approximate. Most of the producing companies have long disappeared and with them their records and much of their product. The Hal Roach Studio records were not available for inspection, and in the case of the early films, many made over forty years ago, the memories of both Stan Laurel and Oliver Hardy were understandably not equal to the task of remembering films that in their own day were regarded by their creators as little more than evanescent cartoons.

STAN LAUREL (alone)
(N.B.: Almost all of the dates are copyright date listings. Production dates in most instances are not available, but it can be assumed that usually only a one- or two-year difference exists between them in instances where they are different.)

NUTS IN MAY	1917
THE EVOLUTION OF FASHION	"
HOOT MON	1918
HICKORY HIRAM	"
WHOSE ZOO	"
HUNS AND HYPHENS	"
JUST RAMBLING ALONG	"
NO PLACE LIKE JAIL	"
BEARS AND BAD MEN	"
FRAUDS AND FRENZIES	"
DO YOU LOVE YOUR WIFE?	"
LUCKY DOG	"
MIXED NUTS	1919
SCARS AND STRIPES	"
WHEN KNIGHTS WERE COLD	"

UNDER TWO JAGS	1920
WILD BILL HICCUP	"
RUPERT OF HEE-HAW (or COLE SLAW)	"
THE SOILERS	1920
ORANGES & LEMONS	"
THE RENT COLLECTOR	1921
THE EGG	1922
THE PEST	"
THE NOON WHISTLE	1923
WHITE WINGS	"
PICK AND SHOVEL	"
KILL OR CURE	"
GAS AND AIR	"
MUD AND SAND	"
THE HANDY MAN	"
SHORT ORDERS	"
A MAN ABOUT TOWN	"
THE WHOLE TRUTH	"
SCORCHING SANDS	"
SAVE THE SHIP	"
ROUGHEST AFRICA	"
FROZEN HEARTS	"
MOTHER'S JOY	"
SMITHY	1924
ZEB VS. PAPRIKA	"
POSTAGE DUE	"
NEAR DUBLIN	"
BROTHERS UNDER THE CHIN	"
SHORT KILTS	"
MONSIEUR DON'T CARE	"
WEST OF HOT DOG	"
MANDARIN MIX-UP	1925
SOMEWHERE IN WRONG	"
PIE-EYED	"
THE SNOW HAWK	"
NAVY BLUES DAYS	"
TWINS	"
THE SLEUTH	"
DR. PYCKLE AND MR. PRYDE	"
HALF A MAN	"
COWBOYS CRY FOR IT	"
ATTA BOY	1926
ON THE FRONT PAGE	"

OLIVER HARDY (alone)

Outwitting Dad (his first film), Lubin, Jacksonville, Florida, 1913.

Series with May Hotaly, comedienne, Lubin, 1914.

"Pokes and Jabbs" series starring Walter Stull, Lubin, 1914-15.

The Paperhanger's Helper, starring Bobby Ray, Lubin, 1915.

Series starring Harry Meyers and Rosemary Theby, Lubin, 1914-15. (Lubin absorbed by Vim Comedies in 1915.)

Spaghetti a la Mode, Charley's Aunt, Artistes and Models, The Tramps, Mother's Child and others in a series with Kate Price, Lubin and Vim, 1915.

Back Stage, The Hero, The Millionaire, Dough Nuts, The Scholar and others in a series starring Billy West, supported by Oliver Hardy and Ethel Burton, Vim, 1916.

The Try Out, Ups and Downs, This Way Out, Chickens, Frenzied Finance, Busted Hearts and others in a series starring Walter Stull and Bobby Burns as 'Pokes' and 'Jabbs' respectively, supported by Oliver Hardy, Spook Hanson, and Ethel Burton, Vim, 1916.

Plump and Runt series intermittently through 1916, 1917, and 1918 with Oliver Hardy as "Plump" and Billy Ruge as "Runt," Vim.

He Winked and Won, starring Oliver Hardy and Ethel Burton, Vim, 1917.

Series of Jimmy Aubrey one-reelers for Mitienthal Brothers, Star Light Studios, Yonkers, N.Y., 1917.

Intermittent free lance work for Pathé Studios, Gaumont Studio, Wharton Studio, Edison Studio, and Vitagraph Studio, New York, 1917-18.

Billy West Comedies as "heavy," New York and Hollywood, 1918. (Note: Billy West Comedies were made successively in Jacksonville, Florida, New York, and Hollywood. The Jacksonville and Hollywood director was Arvid Gilstrom who moved to California at approximately the same time as Oliver Hardy late in 1918.)

The Villain, The Artist, King Solomon, The Chief Cook and others in a series at King Bee Studios, Hollywood, 1918. (All films thereafter made in Hollywood.)

Series at L-KO Studios, 1919.

Played "heavies" in two or three films for Vitagraph starring Earl Williams, 1919.

Jimmy Aubrey Comedies as "heavy" or straight man in two separate Hollywood series. The first series of 12 was directed by Knowles Smith and the second series of 10 was directed by Jesse Robbins, 1919 to late 1921.

Played in several early Buck Jones pictures directed by W. S. Van Dyke at William Fox's Western Ave. Studio, 1920.

The Fly Cop, The Sawmill, Scars and Stripes, The Wizard of Oz, The Girl in the Limousine, Kid Speed and others with Larry Semon, variously produced by Vitagraph, and Chadwick Pictures Corp., 1921-25.

Zenobia, 1939.

The Fighting Kentuckian, 1950.

Riding High, 1950.

The Hal Roach Comedy ALL STARS

(with Laurel and Hardy but not as featured players.)

GET 'EM YOUNG	1926	(Laurel substituting for Hardy.)
SLIPPING WIVES	"	(Their first film together.)
WITH LOVE AND HISSES	1927	
SAILORS BEWARE	"	
DO DETECTIVES THINK?	"	
FLYING ELEPHANTS	"	
SUGAR DADDIES	"	
CALL OF THE CUCKOO	"	
THE RAP	"	
DUCK SOUP	"	
EVE'S LOVE LETTERS	"	
LOVE 'EM AND WEEP	"	
WHY GIRLS LOVE SAILORS	"	
SHOULD TALL MEN MARRY?	"	
HATS OFF	"	

The Laurel and Hardy films. (As stars. Hal Roach Studio, unless otherwise indicated.)

PUTTING PANTS ON PHILIP	1926	(The first "Laurel and Hardy" film.)
THE BATTLE OF THE CENTURY	1927	
THE SECOND HUNDRED YEARS	"	
LET GEORGE DO IT	"	
THE WAY OF ALL PANTS	"	
LEAVE 'EM LAUGHING	1928	
FROM SOUP TO NUTS	"	
YOU'RE DARN TOOTIN'	"	
THEIR PURPLE MOMENT	1928	
SHOULD MARRIED MEN GO HOME?	"	
HABEAS CORPUS	"	

TWO TARS	1928
WE FAW DOWN (also called WE SLIP UP)	"
THE FINISHING TOUCH	"
EARLY TO BED	
LIBERTY	1929
UNACCUSTOMED AS WE ARE	" (Their first sound picture.)
DOUBLE WHOOPEE!	"
BIG BUSINESS	"
MEN 'O WAR	"
THE PERFECT DAY	"
ANGORA LOVE	"
BACON GRABBERS	"
THEY GO BOOM	"
THE HOOSEGOW	"
HOLLYWOOD REVUE OF 1929 (Feature)	"
BERTH MARKS	"
WRONG AGAIN	"
THAT'S MY WIFE	"
NIGHT OWLS	1930
BLOTTO	"
BE BIG	"
BRATS	"
BELOW ZERO	"
THE LAUREL AND HARDY MURDER CASE	"
ANOTHER FINE MESS	"
HOG WILD (also called AERIAL ANTICS)	"
ROGUE SONG (Feature)	"
CHICKENS COME HOME	1931
OUR WIFE	"
LAUGHING GRAVY	"
COME CLEAN	"
ONE GOOD TURN	"
HELPMATES	1931
BEAU HUNKS (also called BEAU CHUMPS)	"
PARDON US (Feature)	"
ANY OLD PORT	1932
THE MUSIC BOX	"
THE CHIMP	"
COUNTY HOSPITAL	"

NOTHING BUT TROUBLE (Feature)	1944	(Metro-Goldwyn-Mayer)
THE BULLFIGHTERS (Feature)	1945	(20th Century-Fox)
ATOLL K (Feature)	1952	(Fortezza Films and Films Sirius)

INDEX

171

Other SIGNET Books You Will Enjoy